On Intimate Terms

On Intimate Terms

The Psychology of Difference in Lesbian Relationships

Beverly Burch

University of Illinois Press *Urbana and Chicago*

For Beverly Elizabeth Wallace Burch,
who wanted me to write a book.

Copyright 1993 by the Board of Trustees of the University of Illinois
Manufactured in the United States of America
C 5 4 3 2 1

This book is printed on acid-free paper.

Library of Congress Cataloging-in-Publication Data

Burch, Beverly.
  on intimate terms:
    the psychology of difference in lesbian
  relationships / Beverly Burch.
        p.   cm.
    Includes bibliographical references (p.   ) and index.
    ISBN 0-252-01801-X (cl. : acid-free paper)
    1. Lesbian couples.   2. Interpersonal relations.   I. Title.
  HQ75.5.B87   1993
    306.76'63—dc20   92-2631
                                                        CIP

74162

Contents

Acknowledgments

Thinking of those who contributed to the existence of this book impresses upon me again that a book or an idea never has one author, that its sources can always be traced in the community of ideas and people that have touched one's life. I am also impressed with the lengthy gestation of such work. I spent several years writing this book, but before that I spent several more years preparing to write it without knowing that I was doing so. I read the literature on lesbians and homosexuality while I studied the literature of object relations theory. I did not foresee that the topics would come together. With friends I talked about lesbian relationships because we had such a great time doing it—we had no direction or purpose in mind. Somehow these separate strands became interwoven, and the ideas of this book gradually took shape.

The women who allowed me to interview them for this project contributed to it immeasurably. They gave life to this work by transforming the abstractions of theory into personal, daily experience. They told me more about my own ideas than I would have ever dreamed. I thank them for their willingness to share the intimate detail of their lives, especially for being so interesting and entertaining that I forgot that such sharing was work.

Formal work on the book began as my doctoral dissertation. I am indebted to the support and contributions of Rosemary Lukton, Judith Schiller, and Diane Elise for getting me through and past this phase of the task. Transforming it from a dissertation to a book that might be of value to readers other than an academic committee required more help, something to get me past my resistence to yet more interviews, extensive rewriting, and then, even worse, making major deletions. Throughout the process, friends, colleagues, and mentors provided what I needed—interest when I was excited about the work and comfort when I was discouraged. They also gave necessary advice and pointed in new directions. The following people discussed ideas, read chapters, gave me resources, or contributed something vital in one way or another: Vivienne Cass, Sheryl Fullerton, Carla Golden, Nina Ham, Mardy Ireland, Deborah Klein, Fran Miller, Jeannie Miranda, Susan Morton, Tom Ogden, Gayle Pearson, Joan Hamerman Robbins, Sandy Tatman, Ellie Waxman, Amy Weston, and Abby Wolfson. I am grateful to Marilyn Johnson, Diane Ehrensaft, and Mary Giles for several readings of the entire manuscript and excellent editorial advice. I appreciate the help of all the therapists who filled out my questionnaire. Thanks, too, to my editor, Carole Appel, for her interest and enthusiasm.

My deepest appreciation goes to Linda Heine, who shared in this book's growth from the early discussions to the hard times of seemingly unending work and through many readings of the manuscript to its completion. She helped me to discover the meaning of these ideas in my own life.

Introduction

Carol and Alix have been involved with each other for seven years. They live together, and together they raise Alix's children from her former marriage. Like many couples, they generally share the same goals and values. Their backgrounds could not be more different however.

Carol was in high school when she came out as a lesbian. She has never been very interested in men. The lesbian community is clearly her home, and she feels alienated from the world of heterosexuality. Alix, on the other hand, was married for ten years and also had other relationships with men. She enjoyed these relationships and thinks of herself as fundamentally bisexual. She feels as comfortable in the heterosexual world as in the lesbian community—that is, she has a sense of simultaneously fitting in and not fitting in to both groups.

Before they met, each woman was looking for someone like herself. When Alix went to women's events and parties, she hoped to find another bisexual woman, someone rather cosmopolitan. Carol, on the other hand, distrusted bisexual women. She did not expect to be attracted to a woman who looked straight to her. Nevertheless, they met at a national conference and almost immediately fell in love. After a year of cross-country flights, Carol moved to the opposite coast to be with Alix. Their relationship has been the most enduring and satisfying one Carol has experienced, and Alix also says that she has never had such a close relationship.

I interviewed Carol and Alix in the process of writing this book. Their story is similar to the stories of many women with whom I talked. They can identify other attractions much more readily than the basic difference in their primary orientations; in fact, they had not thought of it as a primary attraction. If anything, it was primarily a source of trouble. Listening to Carol and Alix talk about their relationship, I heard once again the fascination and the frustration created by such a difference. They could not settle on the meaning of this difference, and they could not leave it alone.

Carol and Alix may not know quite what to make of the fundamental difference between them, but they think it is significant in ways they have yet to comprehend fully. Even with the tension their difference sometimes causes between them, each feels herself to have been profoundly changed in positive ways by their relationship.

By the time I interviewed Carol and Alix, I had encountered such a story often enough in lesbian relationships—in interviews, in my clinical work, and in my own group of friends—to think that their difference might be an important complementary link that many lesbian couples shared. I wanted to understand the phenomenon of complementary bonding more fully. Do we seek certain differences in others? What factors in lesbian psychology make this particular difference important? How does unconscious bonding take place? These questions were the beginning of this book.

To answer such questions I have considered the literature on lesbian couples, gathered impressions from interviews with individuals and couples, thought about my own experiences, and learned from women in my clinical practice. Contemporary psychoanalytic theory has also helped me to reconceive the lesbian bond. I will try to open these questions, to draw on psychoanalytic thought and the experiences of women with other women, and to find a synthesis of these sources. I am looking for a deeper understanding of lesbians and of the transformative power of all relationships. Are lesbian and heterosexual couples fundamentally different, or are relationship dynamics basically the same, whatever their form?

In chapter 1, I consider the importance of perspective: the assumptions one begins with inevitably influence what one sees. Taking heterosexuality as the norm distorts perceptions of homosexuality. Theories also have built-in biases, and using psychoanalytic theory to conceptualize lesbian relationships is both necessary and difficult.

Beginning with chapter 2, I draw upon interviews that help flesh out these differences among lesbians and suggest ideas about complementary dynamics in lesbian relationships. Chapter 2 deals with developmental theories and the differences in the identities and histories of lesbians. This diversity in lesbian lives points toward the salience of unconscious differences that may constitute a sense of oppositeness. In chapter 3, I argue that these differences create a sense of complementarity for many lesbians. The question is, What gives these differences their meaning and power?

Chapters 4 and 5 discuss the contributions of psychoanalysis to understanding unconscious dimensions of relating. Chapter 4 addresses the nature of complementarity: How does a person choose a partner who will complement herself or himself? This issue leads to the question of why people want relationships at all, and what psychological functions relationships serve. Chapter 5 then examines some unconscious processes in bonding and attachment. I discuss unconscious communication as it takes place through projective identification, a means of connection and attraction between people. Projective identification has the capacity to transform or expand the self as well as to deny or defend against undesirable parts of the self.

Chapters 6 through 9 again draw extensively upon the interviews to examine the terms of complementary connections between primary and bisexual lovers. In chapter 6, I discuss the psychosexual significance of the differences of these connections. Chapter 7 explores them as signifiers of opposite ways of dealing with deviance, or with difference itself. This exploration is continued in chapters 8 and 9 through a closer look at the interplay of gender identifications and interplay in lesbian relationships. In chapter 10, I suggest that traditional views of gender dichotomy in lesbian relationships have obscured other interpretations. A reanalysis of *The Well of Loneliness* gives an alternate view of the classic lesbian novel as an example of how such interpretations have determined subsequent cultural awareness.

Other kinds of relationships are considered in similar terms in chapter 11. Are such bonds found in other relationships? Finally, in chapter 12 I explore the clinical implications of these ideas and discuss further directions for research and theorizing. The synthesis I am seeking is an effort to take another step toward understanding women's psychology, lesbian psychology, and the psychology of relationships.

One | Lesbians and Lesbian Lovers: Finding One an Other

Thinking about Love and Lovers

1 This book is about lesbian relationships, especially about their unconscious dimensions—the dynamic forces that attract and hold female partners together. The book is also about relationships in general and the elements that unite people. Is it necessary to make a distinction between lesbian and other relationships? This question pervades the book.

Traditionally, lesbian relationships have been understood (or misunderstood) through comparison with heterosexual ones. Many lesbians think of their own relationships in terms similar to those of heterosexual marriages. Obviously, heterosexual and homosexual relationships share much common ground that can be fruitfully compared. However, lesbian relationships are unlike heterosexual ones in two important dimensions.

First, both partners are female, thus lesbian relationships reflect the desires, values, norms, and problems common to women. Whatever distinguishes women's psychology from men's will in some way distinguish lesbian from heterosexual couples. Second, the culture at large views lesbian relationships as deviant, which they are, in the rather neutral sense of not following the norm—the prescribed choice of opposite-sex coupling. This deviance gives lesbian couples some freedom from traditional expectations of what their relationships should be. They have more room to experiment and may choose alternatives to the socially cherished ideal of a monogamous partnership that lasts a lifetime.

Unfortunately, deviance is not usually regarded in so neutral a light, and homosexual couples are generally viewed as a disturbed version of deviance. Because homosexuality is often considered pathological, even in the absence of symptomatology, any variation from what is established as normal or healthy (usually based on white, heterosexual, middle-class males) becomes evidence of this pathology.[1] Living with the stigma of pathology, however consciously resisted, cannot fail to have some impact upon a couple's existence. This impact may be hard to define. One lesbian couple may cling to the tradition of monogamous marriage in order to deny deviance, whereas another may resist monogamy with a determination that seems reactionary. The meaning of any behavior depends upon both external (cultural) and internal (subjective and idiosyncratic) views of it.

Lesbian Relationships from a Heterosexual Viewpoint

While many subtle distortions are doubtlessly created by comparing lesbian and heterosexual relationships, a major one has already been suggested. If the norm for a healthy relationship is a monogamous partnership that lasts a lifetime, then alternatives to this norm are subject to interpretations of pathology. Clearly, many heterosexual couples (perhaps most) fail to meet this standard in one way or another, but their failure does not become data about the disease of heterosexuality. A common way of stereotyping a minority or deviant group is to ascribe to it characteristics opposed to the majority culture. Depicting lesbian couples as transient and predominantly sexual in nature, with no empirical support for such a picture, is an example of this tendency.[2]

Sigmund Freud argued that monogamy is not a natural choice, but one imposed by the culture, and the enforced restriction of sexual behavior plays a large part in the genesis of neurosis.[3] If one views monogamy as a social requirement for establishing parentage, then lesbians are free from this constraint.[4] When lesbian couples have children together, the principle of biological parentage established through monogamy is meaningless. However, if one understands monogamy (or nonmonogamy) as an individual emotional requirement, then the question of sexual orientation may have little to do with it. In fact, gender may play a more significant role. Some have argued that women require monogamy for their relationships more often than do men. Lesbians are as monogamous as heterosexual women, and striking differences are found among men according to whether they are in relationships with women or with other men.[5]

A variety of models for relationships is needed. Holding one model as the standard leaves almost everyone falling short and becomes a judgment rather than a way of understanding. The "one true love" ideal has fallen on hard times, and for heterosexuals and homosexuals alike, relationships are sequential.[6] They correspond to phases in an individual's life, to changing needs, or to failing ideals; they may carry romantic hopes at one point and practical considerations at another. People often discover their own developmental tasks through the sequence of their relationships. Although many lesbians have lifetime monogamous partnerships, others aspire to this goal but engage instead in a series of relatively long-term relationships. Others may not have this expectation or desire at all.

In studying relationships, I hope to understand what dynamics help a couple stay together in a creative and fulfilling way. However, forces that keep a couple together in an unhappy and stifling union are also apparent. After all, human beings have difficulty managing both intimacy and separateness. It is necessary to keep the influence of social values and judgments in view rather than to substitute them for what is "natural" in human psychology.

Heterosexual Relationships from a Homosexual Viewpoint

Increasing awareness of cultural diversity allows an appreciation of the risks of applying theoretical principles from one culture to another. The distortions generated by looking at minority or "deviant" cultures from a majority or mainstream perspective are especially damaging because that perspective is too easily adopted as the measure of health and virtue. One gains new insights from comparisons and contrasts only when normative judgments are avoided. However, this is not an easy task.

The opposite approach is rarely taken. How often, for example, are white families seen from a black point of view? How much is known about the "blindness" of sighted people from the perspective of those who do not see? Just as children often know things about parents that no one else (even the parent) knows, because their view is from the "underside" so to speak, those who do not participate fully in the dominant culture see it in their own terms. The outsiders make observations from a vantage point that those within lack. These observations provide a correction to mythic notions that the dominant group holds about itself. As James Baldwin wrote, "Whatever white people do not know about Negroes reveals, precisely and inexorably, what they do not know about themselves."[7]

In this same way, a study of lesbians and lesbian relationships casts a different light on women in general as well as on heterosexual relationships. If lesbian relationships are not seen as different from heterosexual ones as a consequence of pathology, then they become a uniquely revealing arena for observing women's psychology in the absence of male dynamics and influences.[8]

Women relate to each other without the constraints or security of established gender roles and dominance hierarchies. Lesbian couples are two-career families. When the partners are parents, they are usually both involved in child care, housekeeping, money-making, and relationship maintenance. When they go out together, one person does not routinely drive the car while the other is routinely the passenger. Interior decorating, cooking and cleaning, taking care of cars and yards, these tasks are shared or assigned according to talent and preference, not gender. Although tasks are rarely managed with absolute equality in any relationship, lesbians generally share the search for equality as a mutually cherished ethic. From these observations, we quickly realize that women may choose more versatile roles than heterosexual norms encourage.

Other, less obvious, dynamics may be observed in lesbian relationships. How are variations in gender possibilities opened up within lesbian relationships? If humans are seen as inherently or potentially bisexual, as Freud and many others have seen them, what happens to the denied aspects of a person's sexuality? In other words, the unexpressed side of an individual's gender identification and sexual object choice, which lesbian relationships live out in one way, different from heterosexual ones, may inform us about corresponding dynamics in heterosexual and gay male relationships. I will explore some of these conscious and unconscious dynamics. Although my concern is primarily with understanding lesbian relationships, not with analyzing heterosexual ones, some conclusions can be drawn about heterosexuality as well.

From a lesbian perspective, some aspects of heterosexual relationships look rather strange and perplexing. The dominance hierarchy that is institutionalized, even at intimate levels, into heterosexual relationships seems unfathomable to women who live largely outside of such a structure. The allocation of roles by gender, regardless of inclination or skill, appears to render individual differences unimportant. Rather than mimicking them, homosexuals have more often been dumbfounded by heterosexual structures; role-playing occurs with humor and a sly awareness of the meaning behind such patterns.

My initial question remains. Are lesbian and heterosexual couples fundamentally different, or are relationship dynamics basically the same regardless of gender or sexual orientation? The truth of either position seems undeniable: something is lost in excluding either perspective. When homosexual and heterosexual couples are contrasted, the great diversity that exists within each group is obscured. When all couples are conceptualized as alike, meaningful differences are lost. A dynamic tension exists between the two positions that does not allow conclusions drawn from either position to stand alone.[9] The answer to the question must remain a paradox: lesbian relationships are fundamentally different from heterosexual ones, and they are nevertheless similar.

Complementary Attractions; or, Who Is One's Opposite?

When a heterosexual perspective is applied to lesbian (as well as gay male) couples, the idea that they must be founded on artificially or pathologically created gender roles is accepted.[10] Sociologists, psychoanalysts, and psychologists have frequently analyzed lesbian relationships along these lines. From the early sexologists at the turn of the century to popular fiction of the 1950s and 1960s, the dominant stereotype of lesbian relationships was a butch-femme couple. Some lesbians identified with this paradigm, however others did not. Even among those who were involved in role-playing, the roles were rarely as rigidly defined or maintained as early researchers like Havelock Ellis or Richard von Krafft-Ebing depicted them.[11] In later chapters I will address questions of gender roles more fully, but here my point is simply to see that taking a heterosexual view of homosexual relationships gives one a distorted perspective.

The dilemma, of course, is how to understand the underlying attractions and ties that hold same-sex partners together. Understanding the attractions at work when two individuals choose each other as romantic and sexual partners is a mysterious matter. What is metaphorically referred to as "chemistry" in common terms is not much better understood in psychological theory. The folk wisdom that "opposites attract" seems to underlie what is claimed to be scientific thinking as well. For example, psychoanalytic theory postulates that object choice rests ultimately on unconscious oedipal ties. But behind the complexity in the psychoanalytic literature about oedipal experience, there still seems to be a sort of default theory that humans are "naturally" attracted to the "opposite" sex. Freud argues that homosexual object choice relies upon cross-gender identification, that is, he could not conceive of attraction to the same-sex parent except in the terms of heterosexuality.[12]

In Plato's *Symposium* Aristophanes relates the myth of primordial beings who are cut in half by the gods and then go in search of their other half. Our own conception of the complementarity of lovers originates in this myth, according to the psychoanalyst Ethel Person: "Plato bequeathed to us the original Western conception of love, that through love one seeks the other half of one's soul, in order to form a union that will make one whole again."[13] Freud referred to this myth as well, but he assumed the two halves created in this division were inevitably male and female. He had trouble conceiving of such complementarity in terms of homosexuality: "The popular theory of the sexual instinct corresponds closely to the poetic fable of dividing the person into two halves—man and woman—who strive to become reunited through love. It is, therefore, very surprising to find that there are men for whom the sexual object is not woman but man, and that there are women for whom it is not man but woman."[14]

Actually, Aristophanes' myth in *The Symposium* states that "in the first place the sexes were originally three in number, not two as they are now; there was man, woman, and the union of the two, having a name corresponding to this double nature." These three types of humans were then divided in half. Aristophanes holds a low opinion of the men and women who came from the androgynous beings (heterosexuals): they are "lascivious" and "adulterous." Those who were once the original woman (lesbians) simply "don't care for men, but have female attachments." Likewise, the men who were once part of the original male being "follow the male," and "they have the most manly nature."[15] Contrary to contemporary views, in this account lesbians are the quintessentially female beings and homosexual men the quintessentially male ones. It is the heterosexuals who are the androgynous beings.

Observing the fate of this myth in its reinterpretation as a template for heterosexuality reveals the biases inherent in modern thinking about human sexuality. In psychoanalytic thinking and elsewhere, homosexuality is an expression of cross-gender confusion. The myth further suggests that thinking of male and female as the only "opposites" also arises out of heterocentric thinking. According to the *Oxford American Dictionary*, the first definition of opposite is "facing," whereas the second is "contrary" or "different." In finding one's opposite, one faces another who expresses some difference significant to oneself. Gender may be a salient difference, but other dimensions of difference may be of equal or greater significance.

This book addresses the question of complementarity in terms other than gender differences. I am concerned not only with the nature of complementarity in certain lesbian relationships, but also with the implications of this perspective for understanding complementarity in any relationship. In lesbian relationships, as in those between gay men, the notion of attraction of opposites requires some rethinking. What would comprise "oppositeness" where there is apparently only "sameness"?

When we observe lesbians and lesbian relationships, however, it soon becomes obvious that their "sameness" is limited to the fact that all lesbians are women. Lesbians as a group are diverse in every imaginable way. Freud recognized the fallacy of the notion that homosexuals are alike in intrapsychic makeup (although he often forgot it), but his followers nevertheless constructed a "unitary theory of sexual perversion" in which all homosexuality could be understood the same way.[16] More recently, some analytic writers have begun to understand the need for a model of sexual development that reflects multiplicity, that explores "homosexualities" and "heterosexualities."[17]

One of the striking differences between lesbians is that between what I would term "primary lesbians" and "bisexual lesbians." Primary lesbians are women whose primary sexual orientation has always been toward other women. They often knew themselves to be lesbian (or at least "different") when they were very young—in early adulthood, adolescence, or even younger. Bisexual lesbians, on the other hand, came to an identity as lesbian later and often felt themselves to be heterosexual first. They may have had significant romantic and sexual relationships with men and may continue to recognize that as a possibility. Both groups of women consider themselves lesbian, both choose women as their partners, yet this fundamental difference exists between them.

This difference is a consequential one and not merely circumstantial. It reflects differences in intrapsychic development as well as interpersonal experiences that shaped each woman psychologically. This distinction holds an unconscious significance for the psyche, making each an "opposite," with a particular psychological appeal for the other. It creates a kind of complementarity that bonds. The salience of sexual orientation to complementarity in relationships (heterosexual as well as homosexual) is the primary concern of this book.

Psychoanalysis and Homosexual Studies

Because I am exploring unconscious dimensions of relationships and psychosexual development, I have drawn upon ideas in contemporary psychoanalytic theory. The British school of object-relations theory, which understands that all human development occurs within the context of relationships, is an essential part of the theory developed here. Analytic ideas about how unconscious communications take place—that is, via projective and introjective identification—were conceived largely within the British tradition. This conception of unconscious communication affords an understanding of how individuals recognize and use their inexpressible differences. It is a vehicle for explaining complementarity.

In classical Freudian theory, a psychological drive is directed toward an "object" (a person or sometimes a thing). The mental representation of the person in an individual's psyche is also called an object. Thus *object relations* became the term for internal, generally unconscious, depictions of relationships between Self and Other. These, in turn, determine the character of one's actual interpersonal relationships. Object relations may therefore refer either to a person's relationships with other people or to a person's psychological structure—which is visibly manifested through relationships with other people. Object-relations theory in psychoanalysis is concerned with the development of the individual's capacity for relationships, but also, conversely, with the development of the individual through interpersonal relationships, especially the earliest ones with parents.

An object-relations perspective theorizes that self and other (and their interrelatedness) are dynamic structures at the deepest level of psychic organization, part of an inborn code by which all perceptions and experiences are mediated and ultimately interpreted. Both inner and outer life are organized in terms of self-and-other relatedness. This theory moves away from the idea that drives determine development or organize psychic life; instead, it is the need and desire for relatedness that organizes psychic life. Such an understanding is particularly appropriate to a psychology of women, as women's psychological lives are so obviously organized around relationships.[18]

Some significant problems are inherent in a psychoanalytic approach. Psychoanalytic (as well as lay) thinking tends to be unable to conceive of homosexual relationships in terms other than those of heterosexuality. Freud's failure to understand the nature of desire that is not based on opposite-gender attraction is emblematic of the narrow range of thinking that has left us with constricted notions of homosexuality. This limitation has led to several basic fallacies, or prejudices, about homosexuality.

First, homosexuality is considered to be pathological per se, simply because it is not heterosexuality. Second, the terms of psychosexual development reflect similar prejudice. Gender identity, sexual preference, sexual identity, and sex-role behavior are practically equated: one is presumed to define the other in consistent ways. Being a genetic female then means being feminine, which in turn means being attracted to men and behaving as a counterpart in the role of wife. Although the cultural changes that have occurred in the expression of these dimensions are considerable, psychoanalytic theory has not fully reconceived either these variables or the interrelationships among them.

In spite of these rather major problems with psychoanalytic theory, it seems impossible to delve into issues of intimacy and sexual development without drawing upon the enormous contributions of psychoanalytic theory. The analytic approach to these complex issues is rich, not only in content but also in its possibilities for reconceiving its own ideas. It seems essential to move beyond the traditional antagonism between psychoanalysis and homosexual studies.

Divergent approaches to homosexuality have coexisted in more or less willful neglect of the insights of each. Biology's pursuit of a genetic or hormonal key, psychoanalysis's clinically based theories, social psychology's research, and sociology's analyses—each discipline ignores or rejects the insights of the other. Their mutual indifference is not surprising considering the chasm between theoretical viewpoints that they encompass.

As discreditors of analytic theory have long pointed out, psychoanalysis focuses almost exclusive attention on internal factors. More relationally oriented schools of analytic theory understand intrapsychic development within the context of interpersonal relating between parent and child. Still, relatively little weight is given to the social and cultural environment that also profoundly shapes personality—that of the parent as well as the child. Cross-cultural studies reveal striking differences in development, as Erik Erikson's work has shown, but perhaps because the task is daunting, these analyses are rarely made.[19] The body of psychoanalytic theory continues to develop with little room for including cultural determinants.

Social psychology and its heirs, such as homosexual studies, attempt to redress this failure, but the social approach has been so critical of the intrapsychic approach that it tends to explore only the more conscious aspects of development, sometimes even denying the role of the unconscious altogether. Social psychologists attend to issues of gender and sex-role identity in terms of socialization, looking not only at the family but also at such other institutionalized influences as school, church, peer group interactions, class, and race. Why do people respond to environmental influences in different ways however? It is necessary to think in intrapsychic terms as well as social ones in order to account for personal differences.

Idiosyncratic dimensions of individual personality are already shaped in important ways before the environment outside the family plays a major role. For this, we must turn back to infant development. Parents themselves function as agents of social institutions, carrying the values and attitudes of the culture at large into the home. Allowance for constitutional differences must be made as well.

With respect to homosexuality, analytic theory has been preoccupied exclusively with the genetic question of how sexual orientation develops. Because this question is almost always framed in terms of pathology, the pursuit is actually one of specifying pathological strains in homosexuality. Psychoanalytic theory ignores homosexual studies and is unconcerned with sexual identity development per se, treating sexual identity as equivalent to sexual orientation. Its course of development and its significance to integrated functioning is overlooked. The role of strong cultural sanctions against homosexuality is almost nonexistent in this analysis.

The field of homosexual studies in turn denies interest in a psychodynamic consideration of the question of etiology. Oddly, this attitude implies agreement with psychoanalysts on this one point, equating the question itself with an assumption of pathology. Homosexual studies all the way back to their roots in the Kinsey Institute research of the 1940s and 1950s set themselves up against psychoanalysis as an alternative approach. In recent decades, homosexual studies have been influenced by the liberation movement. Many writers in this field are gay men and lesbians, who emphasize homosexuality as a matter of personal identity development. Grounded in sociological and social psychological perspectives, they are either antagonistic or indifferent to psychodynamic approaches. Perhaps the original antagonism between homosexual studies and psychodynamic theory required little accommodation of the two to each other. It now seems theoretically wasteful for these various lines of thought to coexist without much interest in or knowledge of the other's development. Each perspective has a contribution to make, and each addresses deficiencies in the other.

The definition of pathology needs to be considered nevertheless. Exactly what a healthy person is, or what defines healthy sexuality, is difficult to state. In general, the answer is framed in terms of two dimensions: the degree of deviation from social norms and the degree of psychological suffering in an individual life. These dimensions are themselves always confounded by cultural values that vary enormously in different societies and at different times within the same society. Whole societies can be seen as pathological, based on political or religious forces that are repellent to those outside (or inside).

What then characterizes a healthy person? This question constitutes a philosophical dilemma that most psychological theories can do little more than recognize. However, it cautions us against an authoritative attitude in descriptions of health and pathology. In this vein, Robert Stoller writes: "Beware the concept 'normal.' It is beyond the reach of objectivity. It tries to connote statistical validity but hides brute judgments on social and private goodness that, if admitted, would promote honesty and modesty we do not yet have in patriots, lawmakers, psychoanalysts, and philosophers."[20]

Some voices within psychoanalytic theory have always acknowledged that clear-cut distinctions concerning health and pathology are difficult to make. Certainly the original Freudian model of "normal" female sexual maturation included a large degree of compromised development. Again, Stoller expresses the problem:

> What evidence is there that heterosexuality is less complicated than homosexuality, less the product of infantile-childhood struggles to master trauma, conflict, frustration, and the like? As a result of innumerable analyses, the burden of proof (providing demonstrable evidence) has shifted to those who use the heterosexual as the standard of health, normality, mature genital characterhood, or whatever other ambiguous criterion serves one's philosophy these days. . . . Thus far, the counting, if it is done from published reports, puts the heterosexual and the homosexual in a tie: 100 percent abnormals.[21]

When we relinquish the focus on who is normal and who is not and instead try to see what works best for a given individual and how we might understand it, we find that homosexuality and heterosexuality both require more exploration. It is within this framework that the present study draws from both psychoanalytic and homosexual studies. Traditional psychoanalytic thinking linked with historical and cultural prejudices about masculinity, femininity, and homosexuality exert a pull of their own, somewhat like a gravitational field. This book is another effort to launch an alternative analysis past the force of that field.

Other Love: Identities and Attractions

2 The idea that homosexuality is a categorical entity rather than a term that covers a widely diverse range of individuals began with the earliest conceptions of homosexuality. These early ideas evidence more of the distortion that originates in a heterosexually centered worldview. In this view, lesbians and gay men are the Other, notable primarily for their lack of heterosexuality. Their differences with each other, and their internal differences within their respective groups, are obliterated.

Further, nothing so clearly illustrates how social norms affect allegedly scientific thinking than the history of theories about homosexuality.[1] The first theories of homosexuality began with the birth of the discipline of "sexology." During the middle of the nineteenth century, psychologists were intent upon establishing psychology as a science, as legitimate and rigorous in its methodology as physics and as capable of being subjected to empirical verification. Sexology was an offspring of this thrust, and it was here that homosexuality first became the object of systematic study. The conservatism of the Victorian period, especially regarding sexual matters and gender roles, further determined the tone and direction of these theories.

The concept of "the homosexual" as a person, a particular kind of person, did not even exist before the work of the sexologists. The term was first used in 1869.[2] Startling as it now is, the fact remains that "the homosexual" is a relatively recent notion, created largely by German and British theorists who wished to make a science of sexual behavior. Same-sex eroticism and relationships have existed in every known culture, but systematic identification of people on the basis of same-sex relations was not thought of. Cultures relatively untouched by modern scientific thought do not conceive of "the homosexual person," yet they tolerate widespread homosexual practice.[3]

As Michel Foucault notes, in the nineteenth century, the homosexual "became a personage, a past, a case history and a childhood, in addition to being a type of life, a life form, and a morphology, with an indiscreet anatomy and possibly a mysterious physiology."[4] As soon as the deviation became a deviant, theories of etiology began to appear. As psychology and sociology became clearly established as academic disciplines, they took up the question of homosexual etiology.

One of the important tasks in writing about homosexuality is to shift the focus from etiology to dynamics, to deemphasize the question, What causes homosexuality? and ask instead, What is homosexuality? and How is it expressed in relationships? When I explore the question of etiology, my concern is for how differences in development play out in the dynamics of relationships, not in what "causes" lesbians to be lesbians.

Again, the problem with the question of etiology is that pathology inevitably seems to be implied. The question from a neutral perspective, as Freud sometimes attempted and sometimes abandoned, must be, What leads sexual interest to be turned in a particular direction, either heterosexual or homosexual? An exclusive preference for either sex requires some explanation. The question is a large one and not adequately answered by any one theory.

Pursuing etiology tends to reinforce the notion that homosexuality is an entity, that it reflects a distinct psychology found in most individuals who choose same-sex partners. Much contemporary thought on sexuality focuses instead on "homosexualities," which manifest a range of internal and external differences.[5] (Heterosexuality includes the same diversity, of course.) Distinctions among lesbians could be made in many ways. The difference that concerns me is expressed most succinctly as a distinction between a bisexually oriented lesbianism and what might be termed a more strictly woman-oriented, or primary, lesbianism.[6]

Primary Lesbians and Bisexual Lesbians

This difference in lesbian orientations is complex and not easy to define precisely. Bisexual and primary lesbians generally, but not always, have different histories in their prior relationships (i.e., whether with women or men). Their experiences in developing a gay identity, and in its final clarity, are usually not the same. Their subjective experiences of fitting conventional roles or identities, especially gender-related ones (i.e., not only femininity but also being able to pass as heterosexual) may also be different.

Some primary lesbians consider themselves to have always been lesbian. Even when very young, they knew their interest was in other women. Some felt they had no sexual identity, a confused identity, or a conflicted one until they came out. They may have had no significant sexual and emotional relationships with men or related to men primarily in an effort to hide or deny their lesbianism. In her study of college women who identified as lesbian, Carla Golden notes:

> Some of these women had from an earlier age (usually between six and twelve) considered themselves to be different from other girls. Whether or not they had a label for it, they experienced themselves as different in that they felt sexually attracted to and oriented toward other girls or women. . . . [T]hey may or may not have had lesbian relationships, and they may even have had heterosexual ones, but regardless, they felt themselves to be different in that they were attracted to females. Furthermore, this was experienced either at the time, or in retrospect, as something beyond their control. . . . Some of these women offered comments to the effect that they were "born" lesbians.[7]

Bisexual lesbians often identify as lesbians later in life. They may have had significant relationships with men. Some marry, some live with men, others have long-term relationships with men with whom they feel they are in love and to whom they are sexually attracted. Often they clearly identify as heterosexual in their early years. Nevertheless, bisexual lesbians discover women as sexual and emotional partners at some point and come to identify as lesbians. Golden notes that even among younger women this distinction prevails. Following Barbara Ponse, she calls this group "elective lesbians" because they think of their sexual preference as a choice:

> Unlike primary lesbians, these women did not have a conscious sense of being different from other girls at a younger age. . . . These women usually had some heterosexual experience as they got older, and even when they had not, they had heterosexual identities. . . . [Some] did not view sexual attraction to women as an essential and unchanging aspect of who they were, although they strongly believed they would continue to have their primary (if not all) relationships with women. Some women said they considered themselves to be lesbians whose sexual

feelings could be most accurately characterized as bisexual, or just sexual.[8]

Some of the women I interviewed for this book distinguished themselves clearly as primary lesbians. Lucy, who identified herself as a "born lesbian," said: "I think that I knew that I was most emotionally—and on some level physically—attracted to women always. I remember knowing that when I was four, maybe five. There was no word for it then, for me. By the time I was ten, there was the word queer, and I knew that was right."

Jan also described her sexuality this way: "I wasn't anything until I was lesbian. I didn't know I was gay, but I knew something was different. During high school I had few boyfriends, and there was no emotional connection at all. I had very close, intense relationships with girlfriends, but they were more one-sided—I felt more intensely than they did. They were crushes, but I didn't see it that way then. I didn't get what the furor about men and boys was. I thought it was just immaturity until after I came out and looked back and could see what it was. Once I met other lesbians, I started having feelings I hadn't had my whole life." For these women, their lesbianism was always primary. Once having relationships with other women became a real option, they never had an involvement with a man again.

Other women I interviewed talked about their relationships with men and women in a very different way. Several had been married, often happily, for a number of years, and they retained an interest in men at some level, even though they all said they would probably never choose a relationship with a man instead of a woman. Maggie, who had been married for twelve years, said: "When I first got involved with women, then I thought I would go back and forth [between men and women]. Now it seems unlikely that I'll ever be involved with a man again. I guess because it feels good to make love to her. . . . that's the bottom line. I'm sure because it works. It also felt good to make love with men though. So maybe I don't know what makes the difference. . . . Identifying as a lesbian is not a big part of it, although I do because that's how I see my future."

Two women said they were still more easily attracted to men than women, but their relationships with women were more satisfying and they preferred women. Fran remembered all of her early attractions as being toward men. She married and had children, but her marriage broke up. A woman began to pursue her. She was interested. "The die was cast at the end of that first relationship. I wonder what would have happened if she had not been aggressive. However, I was suspiciously interested in her lifestyle before she pursued me....I think about it pragmatically now. I like women better."

Some women who might be considered primary lesbians have, perhaps surprisingly, also been married. There are important clues, however, in how these women describe their former marriages. For example, one woman told me that although she had been married for a number of years and had several children, her marriage was a "void," a relationship empty of real emotional attachment for her. She had married because she was unable to conceive of any alternative for herself, economically or socially. When she divorced in her forties, she knew she had been interested in women since adolescence. Bisexual women often describe their long-term relationships with men more positively, as good choices for themselves and sometimes as choices that could conceivably be made again.

To confuse things further, a bisexual lesbian might, for circumstantial reasons, never have been in a relationship with a man. Like the young women Golden interviewed, they may know themselves to be bisexual even without such involvement. Although some writers have made the distinction between primary lesbians and "elective" lesbians, I do not find these terms fitting. Women in the first group sometimes also speak of being lesbian as a choice, although the question of whether one is attracted to certain people and not to others is probably not a conscious choice for anyone. *Primary* and *elective* are terms that make sense only when applied to identity, not to object choice.

No litmus test can certify the distinction between primary and bisexual lesbians. Generally, there are contrary histories; sometimes there are clearly felt and consciously expressed differences; sometimes there might simply be a difference in emotional responses when, for example, a mutual friend falls in love with a man. One woman might understand her friend's experience more abstractly, whereas the other may understand it on an emotional level. Unfortunately for those of us who try to clarify it, this distinction is fluid; the defining principle between primary and bisexual lovers may shift a bit from woman to woman. In an intimate relationship, the distinction may be recognized at both conscious and unconscious levels.

Throughout this book I sometimes distinguish primary and bisexual lesbians through their differences in relational histories with men and women. It is simpler to make this distinction as if it were clear-cut, with easily identifiable characteristics, but it is not. Because social pressures have determined many women's choices, a distinction between primary and bisexual lesbianism can be subjective, a difference expressed as a state of mind more than in behavior. Intrapsychic differences are presumed, but these are always hypothetical. A continuum of experience exists from strictly primary lesbians to women who are clearly bisexual.[9] Most lesbians probably fall somewhere in between.

Identity and Object Choice

Sexual identity is a term with different meanings for different writers. Some use it to mean sexual orientation, some to mean what others would call gender identity, and some share my meaning—a socially constructed identity through which one comes to think of oneself as lesbian, gay, heterosexual, bisexual, or whatever.[10]

A lesbian identity is not necessarily equivalent, however, to desiring involvement with women. Generally, it is equivalent, and both psychoanalytic and common usage tend to assume that it is, but the behavior, fantasies, and desires of many people do not match their identity or self-labeling as heterosexual or homosexual. For example, there is the woman who states, "I'm not lesbian. I just happen to be in love with this woman." Her emotions and attractions are inconsistent with her identity. There is the woman who identifies as lesbian although she is involved in a sexual relationship with a man or is essentially asexual. Likewise, many women call themselves heterosexual yet acknowledge bisexual interests.

By situating oneself in what one might call a homosexually centered reference, one can see how sexual identity emerges as a separate developmental line, distinct from object choice or sexual preference. One then also sees how this distinction applies equally to heterosexual identities. Either lesbian or heterosexual identity is a social construct that incorporates psychological elements.

Psychoanalytic theory has had little concern with the development of sexual identity per se. Instead, it has focused only on object choice. Sexual identity (i.e., identity as homosexual or heterosexual), where this term is used at all, is treated as synonymous with sexual orientation, or, again, object choice.[11] However, identity and orientation are not synonymous; there are bisexual and primary lesbians, bisexual and primary heterosexuals.

Those who understand identity as a social construct point out that to explore the development of sexual identity, we must abandon the idea that it simply flows from a relatively permanent, underlying sexual orientation.[12] If sexual identity is socially constructed and open to change, its development rests upon the social and personal significance it holds for the individual, not on anything fundamental to the organization of sexual desire. This approach does not deny the existence of underlying sexual orientation, but recognizes identity and object choice as independent variables.

Object choice also may be relatively fixed at an early age or, like other psychological structures, it may be open to change over a lifetime. Sexual orientation can be conceived of in at least two ways: not only the dichotomy of male versus female object choice, but also one of "restricted and rigid" versus "open and flexible."[13] Those whose underlying orientation is more rigid will be less susceptible to later influences and interactive experiences. Diane Richardson proposes that we think of orientation and identity development as proceeding on parallel tracks, each influencing and organizing the other. Childhood, adolescent, and adult experiences are then selected or deselected to help organize both desire and identity.

From this perspective, identity and orientation are interdependent — but still somewhat separate — variables. They may be incongruent with each other, as when a woman has a woman lover but still identifies as heterosexual, or a lesbian-identified woman is in a relationship with a man, or a married woman has lesbian interests. The various crises, conflicts, and resolutions inherent in formation of a lesbian identity play their part in shaping adolescent, then adult development. They may also bear upon the partnership of two lesbians.

Many theories attempt to explain the course of development and the significance of sexual orientation and identity. Theories tend to focus either inward or outward; they question what within the individual or within the environment leads toward homosexuality. An overview of these theories helps in understanding the interaction of both influences and having a fuller picture of individual sexual and relational interests.

Intrapsychic Sexual Orientation

Differences in identity and sexual histories between primary and bisexual lesbians reflect differences in both intrapsychic development and social experience. Perhaps most significant is the *interplay* between internal and external experience. Internal factors are comprised of two dimensions, the biological and the psychological. The question of whether there may be a "constitutional" or genetic determination of sexual inclinations continues to be explored by those who are biologically inclined. Freud believed in bisexuality as a constitutional endowment in human development.[14] Richard von Krafft-Ebing, Havelock Ellis, and most of the other early sexologists argued that "inversion" was biologically determined, but lacked scientific tools sophisticated enough to substantiate or disprove this assumption.[15]

Technological advances in biology now permit a scientific pursuit of hormonal or genetic keys that might be a factor in sexual orientation. The search for aberrant chromosomal configurations in homosexuality so far has failed.[16] Hormonal research attempts to link higher prenatal levels of androgens with lesbianism, again on the assumption that lesbianism is linked to masculinity in females. These studies have also yielded no evidence.[17]

As John Money has summarized biological studies:

> There is a possibility that heterosexualism, bisexualism, and homosexualism—maybe transexualism and transvestitism also— are to some degree determined in a rather direct way by the amount of androgenic influence on the brain in prenatal life. If so, then there is no known way of specifying this degree, and the hypothesis itself, though scientifically legitimate, is still largely science-fictional with respect to proof. It is equally feasible to hypothesize that all people are potentially bisexual when born, and that some become postnatally differentiated to become exclusively heterosexual or homosexual, whereas others always retain their original bisexuality.[18]

The biological question is thus unanswered and unanswerable at this point. Freud's original proposition remains a possibility, leaving the field open for social and psychological theories to formulate other determinants.[19]

Psychoanalytic theory emphasizes internal or intrapsychic factors. In analytic thinking, adult relationships manifest internal traces of earlier ones. One's object choice reflects both oedipal (3–5 years old) and pre-oedipal (0–3 years old) experience. Briefly stated, each person experiences both aspects of oedipal love, that is, with both mother and father as desired object. One of these is usually repressed while the other comes to dominate erotic choice in adult life. The repressed oedipal experience generally remains unconscious, disowned in conscious life. Nevertheless, it always persists as a kind of road not taken.

A major problem with the psychoanalytic story of female sexuality is that pathology is ascribed to all psychosexual development for women. The story of female heterosexuality plots a developmental course in which a daughter is saddled forever with a wounded sense of her own gender. Her shift from mother to father as love object is prompted by her irremediable disappointment in her mother's and her own anatomy (i.e., the lack of a penis).[20] The foundation of her heterosexuality is thus her own misogyny.

The assumption of inherent pathology in lesbianism continues despite a great deal of empirical evidence to the contrary.[21] This assumption of pathology is intertwined with other cultural assumptions about the congruence of sexual orientation with gender and sex-role identity along heterosexual lines. An implicit and tautological argument could be paraphrased as follows: A lesbian is masculine-identified because she is a lesbian, and she is a lesbian because she is masculine-identified. Psychoanalysis has remained unconcerned with the many observations of lesbians who do not fit this characterization (frequently found even in psychoanalytic case studies), with defining masculinity in any way that endures through social changes, or with masculinity in heterosexual women.

Psychoanalytic theory also does not explore variations in lesbian women. If female homosexuality inevitably means pre-oedipal fixation on the mother or foreclosure of interest in males, how do we account for bisexual lesbians, women who begin their adult sexual lives with relationships with men but go on to relationships with women, and then may come to identify as lesbian without renouncing their early or continuing interest in men? The "unitary theory of sexual perversion," as Charles Socarides's work has been named, collapses here.[22]

The failure of psychoanalysis to address women's development on its own terms rather than as a variation on male development (the "primacy of the phallus" was how Freud characterized early sexual development) is frequently acknowledged.[23] This failure has distorted efforts to understand lesbianism as distinct from male homosexuality. Further, a revision of analytic formulations must account for the role of social values and experiences in the culture at large as well as within the family.

The traditional explanation of lesbianism is that it is founded on a psychic love affair with the mother, which the daughter never "outgrows." Because the psychic love affair with the father is either never experienced or is closed off for defensive purposes, the basis for romantic and sexual relationships with men has been foreclosed. However, the question that Freud, and many psychoanalysts since, have struggled to answer is why the daughter would ever give up her mother and switch her interest to her father. Boys (heterosexual ones at least) do not make such a switch. This dilemma makes constitutional theories of sexual development appealing.

Nancy Chodorow suggests that the typical oedipal configuration, even for most heterosexual women, is bisexual.[24] She is referring to a relationally oriented preference rather than a sexually oriented one. This distinction may not be particularly meaningful, however, as sexuality is much more likely to be inseparable from relational desires for women than for men.[25]

> A girl's father does not serve as a sufficiently important object to break her maternal attachment, given his physical and emotional distance in conjunction with the girl's desperate need to separate from her mother but simultaneous love for her. While the father in most cases does activate heterosexual genitality in his daughter, he does not activate exclusive heterosexual love or exclusive generalized attachment. This "failure" is because of his own emotional qualities, because he is not her primary caretaker but comes on the scene after his daughter's relationship to this caretaker (her mother) is well established, and because he is not so involved with his children, however idealized and seductive he may be.[26]

Thus when the girl does turn to her father, the turn is not necessarily away from the mother at all. "When a girl's father does become an important primary person, it is in the context of a bisexual relational triangle. A girl's relation to him is emotionally in reaction to, interwoven and competing for primacy with, her relation to her mother. . . . [A] girl retains her pre-oedipal tie to her mother . . . and builds oedipal attachments to both her mother and father upon it."[27]

From this perspective it is much easier to understand that object choice for many women may be a more flexible matter, with much room for later developmental factors to have a significant role. Interactions with siblings, peers, and teachers may play their part. Social and cultural attitudes about sexuality from schools, churches, and the media also contribute. Finally, the circumstances of life can tip the balance. Sexual identity may shift accordingly over a lifetime.

That Freud's version of psychosexual development is fundamentally a psychology of male development is evident in the name given to this period. Oedipus's story is about male experience, a struggle revolving around a father and a son.[28] There is no story for the daughter here. The myth of Demeter and Persephone more aptly describes the daughter's developmental crisis. In this myth the mother-daughter relationship exists first unto itself, without intrusion by the father or the world of men. Demeter as goddess of crops and Persephone as goddess of the spring are united in innocence and joy until Persephone is abducted and raped by Hades. Persephone lives in the underworld until her mother at last finds her and secures her release. However, before she returns to her mother, Persephone eats the six pomegranate seeds of Hades, half knowing, half forgetting that this act will require her to return to Hades six months of each year.[29] The story describes how the male's entry breaches the exclusive nature of the mother-daughter bond; henceforth the daughter's existence moves back and forth between the mother and the father. Her dilemma is that of a divided psyche, oscillating between two worlds.

Some accounts of the myth emphasize the daughter's sorrow at separation from the mother, others point out her complicity in it. The different emphases simply reflect the dilemma of female experience, expressing both the wish to separate and the wish to keep the mother. Fluctuations between oneness with the mother and separation from her, and movement between the world of the mother and the world of the father, characterize female development and female sexuality in broad terms.

Establishment of object choice is more complex than the oedipal resolution conceptualized in traditional analytic theory, and more than one route exists for determining one's final object choice.[30] For primary lesbians, resolution of psychosexual development may leave intact a female object choice based upon the oedipal mother. For bisexual lesbians, both mother and father may figure prominently. The outcome of this developmental period is likely to be a consequence of interaction between inborn codes of preference with interpersonal experience within the family, none of which are necessarily pathological.[31]

The degree of fluidity or rigidity to this resolution leaves the girl more or less open to later experiences outside the family. In the case of bisexual object choice, the sex of the partner eventually chosen may be especially affected by external, situational influences because intrapsychic requirements are somewhat flexible. Development of sexual identity will then occur in tandem with life experiences and the relative strength of one's interest in men or women.

Social Theories and Sexual Identity Formation

Behaviorism, social psychology, and sociology have also put forward ideas about human sexuality, each from their own perspective. These disciplines criticize the intrapsychic focus of psychoanalysis. They contribute toward a view of homosexuality as not intrinsically pathological, and they move away from the idea of a "homosexual personality." Nevertheless, they also tend to be concerned primarily with etiology and to neglect other questions.

Behaviorists focus upon the circumstances that may have conditioned and reinforced sexual choices. In their view, positive same-sex or negative opposite-sex experiences, with reinforcing circumstances at critical periods, are the determinants of homosexuality.[32] Sociologists and social psychologists are interested in the enormous diversity of sexual patterns, observing the shifts that sometimes occur over the lifetime of an individual. They argue that too many people show a range of sexual behaviors and desires for distinct categories to be created. The Kinsey researchers accounted for homosexuality in social terms: "Exclusive preferences and patterns of behavior, heterosexual and homosexual, come only with experience, or as a result of social pressures which tend to force an individual into an exclusive pattern of one or the other sort."[33] Through psychological tests and empirical data, social psychologists have established that homosexuals are as psychologically healthy as heterosexuals.[34]

The field of homosexual studies arose out of this background and began to consider how it is that some individuals come to identify as homosexuals whereas others do not, even though they may be involved in same-sex relations. Homosexual studies also address such issues as cultural contributions to homosexual experience and the characteristics of homosexual relationships. This work has established the process of coming out as a major developmental event for lesbians and gay men. However, models of identity development tend to assume that homosexual identity begins to be formed early, often in adolescence, and follows a fairly straightforward path unless a defensive retreat is made.[35] Because of this assumption, the interaction of other developmental events with those of identity formation is overlooked.

The experience of coping with an identity labeled deviant by one's society is quite different for adolescents than for people who change identity as adults. During adolescence other issues of social identity are being negotiated as well, and it is a time of great vulnerability. As Erik Erikson notes, "in puberty and adolescence all sameness and continuities relied on earlier are more or less questioned again. . . . The growing and developing youths . . . are now primarily concerned with what they appear to be in the eyes of others as compared with what they feel they are."[36] He reminds us that adolescents are often "clannish" and "cruel" about differences, preoccupied with in-group and out-group status. They may rely upon stereotypes to deal with deviations in social behavior. In this context, coping with a deviant identity is likely to be painful and thoroughly conflicted. Women who come out as adolescents face this formidable challenge.

Fundamental questions such as, What kind of person am I? and

Who are my peers? are challenging for all adolescents, but the challenge is much greater when the answers are unacceptable to one's peers, family, and the society at large. Confronting these issues requires a degree of ego strength that is sometimes beyond an adolescent, and temporary defenses such as negation of one's orientation, social withdrawal, or living some kind of double life may be employed.

Women who come to an identity as lesbian later in life have probably negotiated other issues of social identity. Their assumption of a deviant sexual identity is more like a choice than an inevitability. They may have established a sense of self as relatively "normal," fitting in with the mainstream, at least in terms of their sexuality. Embracing a lesbian identity at this stage means coping with somewhat different issues. It may involve some loss of acceptability and social ease, however the loss of something one has had is a quite different experience from never having had it.

The presence of social support systems has been highly significant for women who come out later in life.[37] Specifically, the emergence of a visible gay community and the support of feminist ideology has provided a positive context for later development that was either missing or not relied upon by women who came out during adolescence. Women who come out later have frequently already altered their ideas about homosexuality, either through positive contact with gay people or exposure to the liberation movements. What may be the hardest part of the task of identity formation (reevaluating lesbianism toward a more positive view) has been dealt with to some degree *before* these women considered the personal significance of homosexuality. Their transition to a lesbian identity can be considerably smoother than that of primary lesbians.

An important difference between the two groups may be found in the sense of self as deviant. The identity of women who begin to think of themselves as lesbian very early in life is likely to include undesired feelings of being different, not in the mainstream, not typically feminine, and, often, not normal. Women who have previously thought of themselves as heterosexual or even bisexual have experiences that are somewhat closer to the mainstream culture. Their participation in heterosexual relationships has been authentic to a large degree, and they may more easily identify themselves as feminine. The change of identity does not carry the same significance for the totality of their identity as it does for primary lesbians, allowing them to feel less different, more normal.

On the one hand, the identity of the primary lesbian may be consolidated clearly as lesbian, but it is more likely to include a sense of self as deviant even after a positive reevaluation of homosexuality is made. On the other hand, the identity of the later developing lesbian may never be as clear. Although she comes to identify herself as lesbian, some confusion, ambivalence, or doubt may persist. At the same time, she may think of herself as more normal, less deviant, than the primary lesbian. Indeed, she may always hold out some part of her identity as nonlesbian because of, or even to preserve, this sense of normalcy.

Those who study the development of a gay or lesbian identity have tended to assume a fairly uniform progress through stages of development.[38] They take little account of differences in the experience of identity development at different ages and in tandem with other developmental experiences that may be occurring simultaneously. Vivian Cass notes that the process may begin at any age and that an individual's age "has considerable influence on his/her mode of coping with the developmental process,"[39] but she postulates that everyone begins with an identity that is "nonhomosexual and heterosexual." In fact, women who come out early often do not begin with heterosexual identity at all. They describe themselves as "born lesbians," "always lesbian," or lacking a specific sexual identity until they become aware of homosexuality.[40] Coping with a sense of differentness and finding a social place for themselves has been an issue from an early age. The distance between these two routes is thus considerable.

The distinction between primary and bisexual lesbians suggests very different paths by which women may have arrived at sexual identity. Women in the first group began to identify themselves, however tentatively, as lesbians at an early age, often by adolescence. Those who have written about their identity development in early years provide a sense of this experience. For example, "The day I accepted my label I still didn't know the word lesbian. The label I accepted was homosexual. Still, I had problems with even that since what little I could find in the literature that was available to me in 1950 was about men or about women in prison. Since neither of those categories included me I concluded that I had to be what I had suspected all along—I was alone in my affliction—so horribly deviant there were no others like me." Another describes her teenage years. "My adolescence was very lonely. I read a lot, never dated (even once), and spent my time mooning over one teacher or another. I knew I was supposed to be having crushes on boys so I went to the library and read everything I could on 'sexual deviance' (that's where the card catalog made you look if you looked under homosexuality). I decided I was gay, though I called it being a 'homo.' "[41]

Accounts of identity development by women who came out later in life, after heterosexual experience, often differ in the extreme. "At my age [50] I consider it expedient to be a lesbian. It's a smart choice for me. . . . So when I say I'm a lesbian, I'm saying that I choose to relate to women at this time in my life and that I'll probably continue to do so. But I'm not closed to relating to a man again. I'm certainly not. At the same time women who have always been lesbians, real lesbians, absolutely fascinate me. . . . You may not agree with me, but I think there is really something different about them."[42]

Another credits the women's movement with allowing her to turn toward women:

> I had become close to the women's movement. . . . It started as kind of an intellectual statement I made to myself. I felt so comfortable with women and was really turned on by the exciting changes I saw in women around me—they certainly seemed to be changing and growing a hell of a lot more than the men of my acquaintance. I began thinking, well—what is so terrible? . . . why not express my feelings sexually with a woman? . . . It so happens that for me—I find relationships with women to be much more equal and free. . . . For me it started off as an idea that progressed to experience and now, I would say, is probably the way I'll live my life.[43]

These striking differences also appeared in some of the interviews I conducted. For example, Lucy was expelled from a private boarding school two weeks before graduation because her relationship with another girl was discovered. The experience left her traumatized about her identity. She, too, learned about homosexuality from the "deviant behavior section of psychology and hygiene textbooks" and decided that didn't fit her: "So there wasn't anything I could identify myself as. I saw it like this, 'Yeah, there's that. . . . But it can't be true. . . . But I'm in love with Roxanne.' So I was in a lot of denial. I think being expelled from high school and having that come up right in my face was very frightening. I had no role models. I was a pariah in high school because of my lesbianism (or my homosexuality as I think it was called then by the teachers, by the mothers, by the other kids). I think that was very, very hard for me." She began to have relationships with men until she moved after college to New York in the early 1970s and discovered the gay pride movement.

Paula, who has never been involved with men, described her first awareness of her sexuality: "I remember when I first realized I had fallen in love with a woman. I was riding on public transit, and I actually broke out in a cold sweat. I thought 'Oh my God, I'm a lesbian.' I had so much negative reinforcement in my family about what a lesbian was and no role models at all that I really felt I might as well be dead."

On the other hand, Fran, who came out when she was forty-three, after sixteen years of marriage and three children, said that for her there was little conflict. It was largely a matter of "getting used to it, finding out there weren't so many problems as expected, and waiting for the dust to settle." She is still attracted to men as well as women but thinks women are a better option. She feels lucky to be so free of homophobia and to have a choice.

Other bisexually inclined women whom I interviewed also found the transition to be fairly easy. Marty, who had almost married one of the two men with whom she had serious and lengthy relationships, found herself socializing primarily with a group of women at her university. They seemed more like herself than any other group of women she had known. Only later did she discover that they were lesbians. "When one of them was nice enough to tell me they were lesbians, at first I thought, 'Well, that has nothing to do with my sexuality.' But it was very soon after that that I got involved with a woman. I don't remember it being conflicted at that time. In fact I felt sort of like I'd found a home, that I was actually very much like the women and that seemed very nice. They were women who wanted the same things I did, who were ambitious. I liked them a lot, so it felt great. The only conflict I had was about my parents' reaction."

These responses reflect the significant differences that exist in lesbian development. Primary lesbians often felt their sexuality to be a given; others saw it as a choice. Again, the possibilities in choice of erotic partners may be relative rather than absolute (after all, something drew the latter group to other women and allowed them to rethink their possibilities), but clearly some women feel greater flexibility or fluidity in sexual choice than do others.

Integrating Psychodynamic and Social Theories

What is needed from an integration of theories is a deeper look at the interaction between internal and external processes. This interaction will always be complex and never easy to specify, but the effort can yield a greater understanding of the vicissitudes of psychosexual development. Identity formation is a variable experience that at one extreme is highly conflicted and even traumatizing; at the other extreme, it is a relatively smooth, ego-syntonic unfolding of awareness in which confrontation with the painful effects of social disapproval is minimal. The distance between these extremes can only be accounted for by the interaction of identity development with other developmental issues, both determining them and being determined by them.

The internal determinants are the early developmental achievements that contribute to ego strength, self-esteem, ability to face reality, and comfort with individuality. These attributes grant more or less flexibility and strength in coping with difficult tasks. External determinants include the social era, the values of one's family of origin and the nature of one's community. These will determine how difficult the task of identity formation is. A small-town environment will present one set of problems and advantages, whereas a cosmopolitan one will present another. A family holding deep religious beliefs that denigrate sexuality will provide a different environment from one with liberal beliefs. The presence or absence of support systems or of respected individuals who identify as homosexual are important variables.

Cass suggests that one's ability to move through the stages of homosexual identity development rests upon an ability to tolerate being different and to resist the pressure of social norms.[44] This indicates how the sexual identity formation process may interact with other developmental accomplishments, especially differentiation of self and other and establishment of a secure, positive social identity. The events of the coming-out process have an impact on such other aspects of development as self-esteem, ambition, autonomy, capacity for relatedness, and interdependence. An integrated identity relieves one from excessive defensive maneuvers and is itself a foundation for further growth.[45]

Understanding the complementarity that exists between primary and bisexual lesbians requires such an interactional approach. Interplay between lesbian partners is determined by differences in such fundamental variables as sexual orientation and sexual identity development. Classical analytic theory tends to ascribe to the primary lesbian more difficulty with tolerating differences because of her inadequate separation from her mother.[46] Cass turns this idea around, however, by pointing out that lesbians who establish a positive sexual identity early in life have a greater ability to tolerate differences than those who are unable to do so, perhaps more than "normal" adolescents who cling to conformity. The ability to overcome social disapproval and formulate a favorable sense of self that includes a "deviant" sexuality is a developmental triumph indicating a high degree of ego strength.

The interplay among these factors has not been articulated properly.

Many variables and great complexity of potential for interaction make the task daunting. In the arts, in personal accounts, and in clinical descriptions are found an infinite variety of individual experience. As theoretical sophistication grows, however, the ability to synthesize these different perspectives will also be enlarged. Psychodynamic theory must develop a greater comprehension of how social meaning contributes to internal experience, and homosexual studies need an early developmental basis for approaching adult growth. These integrations could grant a more sophisticated appreciation of the varieties of sexual expression.

The Road
Not Taken

3 Theories about sexual identity and object choice development suggest the diversity among lesbians. All women who call themselves lesbians share an identity, but they do not necessarily share the same desires, fantasies, and inclinations, nor do they have the same history. Some feel their internal experiences are more bisexual in nature, some feel theirs are more truly woman-centered. This is a difference that matters.

From clinical work, from personal experiences, from discussions with colleagues and friends in the lesbian community, and from thoughts about the popular literature on lesbian couples, I have come to believe that a special attraction often exists between primary and bisexual lesbians. None of these sources provides any hard data, of course. In fact, I've found little data that either support or challenge the idea, a problem that reflects how rarely questions have been asked about dynamic aspects of lesbian relating. (There are few explorations of dynamic complementarity in heterosexual relationships either.) But the more subjective evidence was intriguing enough that I began to explore the nature of this attraction. My ideas about the conscious and unconscious aspects of a bond between primary and bisexual lesbians form the core of this book.

A Pattern of Attraction

To develop this theory further, I interviewed a small group of lesbians, eight individuals and eight women in couples. Such a small group of women could offer little validity to the theory, but their experiences could help me to understand lesbian complementarity and to describe it more fully. The interviews gave me an opportunity to explore in an informal way the observations made in clinical practice. Clinical work does not allow the active exploration that I needed to do, but the interviews did. I wanted to record observations individual women had made about their own course of development and about their relationships.

The women I interviewed were contacted through social and professional networks. I wanted equal numbers of women who identified as bisexual and primary lesbians (four of each) and four relationships that included one of each (again, the subjects were preselected in this way because I sought descriptive data rather than proof). Because I needed a group of women with sufficient life experience behind them to reflect upon these differences, I also chose women who were older (from thirty-five to fifty-two) than Carla Golden's college-age subjects.

When I planned the interviews I anticipated that it might be a delicate matter for some women to define themselves one way or the other or even to choose a third option ("neither description fits"). Because lesbianism is itself inevitably a value-weighted categorization, individual lesbians and the communal norms of lesbianism could make either designation more desirable to one woman, less desirable to another, depending on her own political and emotional biases. For example, some lesbians do not consider bisexual women or women with heterosexual histories "real lesbians" regardless of what they call themselves. Therefore, some women might hesitate to name themselves bisexual. Other women may feel that being a lifelong lesbian is admitting to some limitation, or that being a "real lesbian" is more stigmatizing than being a lesbian with bisexual potential.

To try to minimize these effects as much as possible, I structured the interviews to address differences in several dimensions rather than to rely strictly upon labels. The interviews explored each woman's identity (what she actually called herself—lesbian, gay, bisexual, or whatever), her history of relationships and attractions (whether with women exclusively, or both men and women, as well as subjective experiences or fantasies of being with both), and her thoughts about differences between primary lesbians and bisexual ones. I also asked for thoughts or images of lesbians who fit a category other than her own, views about the meaning of these differences in relationships, and ideas about gender-related topics such as butch and femme lesbians and relationships. Specific questions and the format used in these interviews are given in Appendix A.

My concerns about the difficulty of discussing these matters did not seem founded. Most of the women responded easily and with great interest to all of the questions I asked. Most had little trouble designating themselves one way or the other. I think the relative ease with which they talked openly about such issues is a measure of how much an earlier rigidity in the lesbian community (the need to be "politically correct") has relaxed. In fact, several women commented upon this change, remarking that five years earlier such an interview would have been more difficult and maybe produced different answers. (This is not to say, of course, that the current responses are the more accurate ones. Any qualitative study explores subjective experience that is always in flux, and the concepts of accuracy or right answers are meaningless.) The women's ages may also have contributed to relaxation about these issues. The need to conform to a communal standard is not so pressing for adults in middle-age as it is for adolescents and young adults who are still developing an identity.

On many occasions the women whom I interviewed commented that they had never thought about certain questions I was asking or about the significance of these differences in their relationships. Several said something like "I think this difference is very important in our relationship, but I haven't thought about it and I don't know how to articulate it." At other times women let me know that they were thinking while they were talking, that they were not sure themselves what they were going to say. They were putting new ideas together during the interview and reaching some new awareness of their own experience. In two of the couple interviews, the partners surprised each other with complementary answers as they explored a previously unexpressed dimension of these differences. Sometimes women said that they were sure they would continue to ponder these questions. Eventually, I regretted not having planned second and third interviews and getting the benefit of further thoughts. Nonetheless, I was greatly impressed with the subjects' honesty, perceptiveness, and spontaneous recognition of the issues. Their ability to open new areas of insight quickly and creatively made the interviews exciting and often enjoyable.

I also surveyed therapists who work with lesbian couples (Appendix B). Were the couples in their practice different in their sexual orientation, or were they more alike? This survey gave me further information about the connection between bisexual and primary lesbians: a pattern of relationships indeed emerged between women with different sexual histories.

This pattern of complementarity between primary and bisexual lesbians is hardly inclusive—there are certainly other kinds of complementarity in lesbian relationships—but it seems to occur with some frequency. Because there is no such thing as representative data from a hidden population, we cannot know with any assurance how widespread such a pattern may be.[1] We can only observe its recurrence in relationships that are openly identified as lesbian. In studies of lesbian relationships, information about partner choice or sexual histories is almost always missing. Although the literature on lesbian relationships contains some suggestive accounts, the data are so scarce that these illustrate the pattern rather than establish its frequency.

Evidence from my clinical work with individual lesbians suggests not only that differences exist in sexual histories of lesbian partners, but also that these differences are sources of fascination, disturbance, appeal, and threat. A woman might report that her partner had been a lesbian "all her life," while she herself was newer to relationships with women. Another would relate that her partner had been "seriously involved with men." Such disclosures were given spontaneously, and their significance might easily have been missed except for the tone or particular inflection with which they were expressed. They conveyed experiences of mingled anxiety, awe, alienation, intrigue, or pointed interest. These emotions sometimes recalled the way heterosexual clients, both men and women, spoke of differences with their partners, differences ascribed to gender.

Differences were most apparent when they were most extreme, for example, when one partner had no sexual/romantic interest in men and the other had been happily involved with a man or men. Some lifelong lesbians talked about often being interested in women who appeared to be straight but perhaps were not. This interest could be interpreted in various ways, but it seemed to suggest a sense of the perhaps-heterosexual women as Other.

Differences were usually more subtle, however. For example, in cases in which both women had previously been involved with men, those relationships were experienced very differently. The first woman might feel that her relationships with men had either been false or relatively unimportant, whereas her partner felt that her heterosexual experiences were serious and authentic.

On the other side of this difference, a woman might recognize that her underlying sexuality was rather bisexual even though she identified herself as lesbian. This was clearly distinct from her partner, and the difference was not necessarily a comfortable one to either woman. There was always the threat of renewed interest in men, but something other than that threatened as well, something about how the women were fundamentally different. One case in particular pointed to the significance of this difference. A woman bisexual described having felt some attraction to heterosexual women friends all her life, but usually the attraction was vague and easy to overlook. When she felt drawn to a woman who was clearly lesbian, something shifted internally. She was frightened by and also drawn to that other world. The attraction became focused and compelling.

A significant feature of these differences in actual relationships was the fascination they held for the individual women. One woman whose partner had come out while a teenager, reported that she never tired of hearing what it was like being with women at such a young age. A lifelong lesbian liked to question her partner about what it was like to be in love with a man. Was it the same? How could it be? Their interest seemed to go beyond the usual interest lovers have in each other's past love affairs. It seemed to be intrinsically tied to the sex of the former partner. In the first case, there was a hunger to know what that early world of female love was like. In the second, there was a sense of trying to comprehend the incomprehensible. The affective charge, both positive and negative, attached to these differences alerted me to their significance. As always in clinical work, the threatening nature of an emotional response signals deeper roots in unconscious meaning.

Once this pattern had suggested itself, it began to be apparent in other quarters as well. Observations made within the lesbian community, conversations with colleagues (some of whom worked extensively with lesbians in therapy), and informal talk among lesbian friends affirmed it as an unnamed but easily recognized pattern, one that might have dynamic implications. In this sense it seemed to be a matter of "pretheoretical" or "tacit knowledge." As Marcia Salner explains it, this is knowledge that "participants in a communal existence" carry, that which is known but has not yet been articulated.[2] The picture that began to come into focus was that many lesbian relationships show some meaningful (*meaningful* is a highly subjective term, designated as such by the individuals themselves) degree of this difference in underlying sexual orientation, as reflected in differences in past relationships, clarity of identity as lesbian, or sense of self in relation to heterosexuality.

Some relationships do not show this difference. For example, early relationships between young women seem less likely to be founded on such a difference. This can be understood in at least two ways. The first explanation is practical: being young, the women generally knew themselves to be lesbian rather early and had little experience with men. (Some do go on to a chiefly heterosexual life later, however). Second, there may be a strong need to affirm one's identity as lesbian by finding a partner who reflects and reinforces it through her own experience. Later, as personal identity is consolidated, the need for a partner who mirrors one's own experience may decrease. In other cases, older women who have both had traditional, married heterosexual experiences become involved. Here may also be a need to confirm each other in a life-changing decision. Sometimes when these relationships end, the women make different choices and seek partners who have a different history.

Some relationships seem to be founded upon dynamics outside the scope of this study. One bisexual woman, Fran, reported that it was important for her to find a partner who was not deeply involved in lesbian experience and community. She lived in a primarily heterosexual world and needed someone who would fit into that world with her, had long-term relationships with men, and was not strongly lesbian-identified.

With the exception of Fran, the individuals I interviewed saw differences in their own histories and those of their partners, some more striking than others. Six of the remaining seven identified their current partner as meaningfully different from themselves in either the presence or absence of relationships with men. For example, I asked Lucy whether her lovers had a history different from her own. "Oh, I think a different one! I sure have had these conversations with women I've been with. The person I've been with now for about twelve years identified herself as heterosexual. Her relationships had all been with men, and she hadn't applied any of those words [gay, homosexual, lesbian] to herself or to her thoughts either."

Paula, a primary lesbian, said, "I've generally been involved with women who had a very different path.... One of my main relationships was with a woman who decided politically it was important to be with women.... I mean she *worked* to change her idea of a sexual partner. It certainly didn't come from the same place it came from in me—that I *have* to be. And that was pretty remarkable to try to understand, to get my mind around what that would be like." Dina, also a primary lesbian, commented that she had often been with women who were coming out or who had only been with one other woman. "My partners have had extensive heterosexual pasts. I'm attracted to women who are different. There has been something soothing about them. I've never been involved with an 'old time dyke,' which I think I border on, myself."

Maggie, a bisexual lesbian, had been married for twelve years and was involved with a woman who had never had a serious relationship with a man. She felt this was the most significant difference between them: "There are all these differences. She's not Jewish, I am. We have class differences. But basically I feel the greatest difference is the one in our sexual histories. I feel it's a cultural difference as much as being Jewish. . . . It's a really major difference and really relevant to our lives." Wendy, another bisexual lesbian, had been married twice and raised a child. In her forties now, she had been with a woman for five years who had a primary lesbian background. She experienced differences with her lover in several ways. For example, even after she came out, she could pass as straight, whereas her lover definitely looked like a lesbian. "We talk about this off and on, especially what it was like for her. The discrimination, the repercussions. I am very aware of what that felt like, that censure. It just feels like we are different. We are not so much the same. . . . And, being a late-comer, I think it's reassuring to me to be with someone with knowledge and experience I haven't had."

For Marty, the other woman in the individual interviews, the difference with her partner was more subjectively apprehended. Their histories were not as different, yet she felt their potential for authentic bisexuality was different. Sometimes she emphasized the reality of this difference, and sometimes she minimized it. "She was involved with men, but never had a committed relationship with a man, never saw them frequently. I would put her more on the lesbian side—even though it took her a long time to figure out she was a lesbian. I'm not sure. I think I am more attracted to men sexually, and she isn't so much. I don't know. Maybe I like us to be different."

The four couples chosen showed definite differences in their histories. Carol and Alix, whose story introduced this book, had been together for seven years. Alix was married for ten years and had two children. She had enjoyed sex and love with men, whereas Carol had never been interested in men. Janine and Karen had also been together for seven years; Janine came out at thirty-five, after thirteen years of marriage. The marriage was a good one, but toward its end Janine felt a growing interest in women. She found it hard to leave because she loved her husband; it took five years "to get clarity." She is clear that she will continue to be with Karen. Karen came out at twenty-five however, and it was no surprise to her:

KAREN: Absolutely not, I'd been denying it for a long time, for years and years. It was always there for me, but unconsciously.
JANINE: It would be hard for me to say that.

The other two couples were similar. Both involved one woman who identified herself as a primary lesbian and another who had been extensively bisexual. Ellen, who had been with Miriam for nine years, said she has always been attracted to women and never particularly attracted to men. She had a casual relationship with a woman in college, then fell "seriously in love" with another. Their relationship was closeted, and she did not identify as a lesbian. She tried being with men after that, hoping "there would be a little spark." When that did not work, she sought out the lesbian community. Miriam, her opposite, was engaged to a man when she had a brief affair with a woman just to feel she was "sexually liberated." The engagement ended, she moved to California, and was involved with both men and women for a number of years, still thinking she would marry eventually. Although she identifies herself as a lesbian and is extremely committed to her relationship with Ellen, she cannot say that she has no sexual interest in men.

Abby and Suzanne had been together for five years. Suzanne was ten when she had her first experience with another girl, an involvement that lasted four years. Although she dated boys for awhile in high school, she continued secret affairs with girls and had many struggles about gay friends with her mother. Suzanne did not identify herself as a lesbian until she was in her early twenties, but sexually and emotionally the die was cast much earlier. Abby's history is different. She came out in her late twenties after a period of involvement with both men and women. She kept weighing the question, Am I looking for a relationship with a man or a woman? at every turn. Then she met Suzanne, and "everything felt right." Still, Abby adds that if she were no longer with Suzanne, she would probably explore a relationship with a man again.

None of these women thought their relationship with a woman who had such a different orientation to lesbianism was coincidental, yet they could not find the underlying meaning of it. Karen and Janine discussed their mutual interest in their different histories.

KAREN: Everyone I've ever been with was with men. Absolutely, they were all fence-sitters. . . . I'm attracted to women who have that broader range of experience, including being with men.
JANINE: But they were also ambivalent about men. They couldn't really commit themselves.
KAREN: Yeah, that was the problem. That was the downside.
JANINE: I liked your background. I think there was an element of

wanting someone more experienced in being with women. I knew I didn't want someone ambivalent about being with a woman. . . . It was interesting, intriguing. We spent a lot of time talking about your past relationships. Why you got involved, what they were like. I knew you were a real lesbian. There was some complexity about you that made it interesting. And you liked that I'd been in such a long-term relationship.

KAREN: But because it was with a man.

JANINE: But you liked that *permanence*, that ability to commit.

KAREN: Yes, but being married to a man for thirteen years is something I know nothing about. It's more interesting than a few years with men before coming out at twenty-five, like me.

Suzanne and Abby also discussed the issue.

SUZANNE: It's not an accident. I don't believe in "accidents" like that.

ABBY: Well, I needed to be with a woman who wasn't wishy-washy about her sexuality. The fact that you were clear about that was very important to me. I'd been with women who were more like me and were unsure sometimes, and it consumed the relationship.

SUZANNE: I view it as interesting . . . because it's different. How we were with men is very different, both socially and sexually. It doesn't bother me that that's who you are because I have a lot of trust in your commitment. . . . It's just more interesting.

Studies of Lesbian Couples

Recent literature on lesbian couples does not provide real evidence of this pattern but again illustrates it. Betty Berzon notes the difference in her own fifteen-year relationship:

My partner and I are about as different as two people can be. I come from a Midwestern, middle-class Jewish family. She comes from an East Coast, working-class Italian Catholic family. My parents are divorced, and I have had five stepmothers. Her parents, on the other hand, were married to each other for over fifty years.

I have struggled with my sexual identity for most of my adult life, coming out after I was forty. She knew she was a lesbian at an early age and has never tried to be anything else. I have had more romantic liaisons with men and women than I can possibly remember. She has had two relationships, one with me and one with her former (female) lover of twelve years.[3]

In this list of differences, those of the first paragraph are common to many types of relationships. Those of the second paragraph are significant for lesbians. Berzon seems to acknowledge its special place here.

In the only example of complementarity, or "completion fantasies" as she calls them, between lesbians, Berzon describes a primary lesbian who "still carries with her the pain of an adolescence in which she felt different from the others." This woman enters a relationship with another, a "prom queen" type. Berzon notes that in this affiliation, the first woman "in a sense borrows that aspect of [the other's] identity, and the longstanding pain of her teenage years is somewhat ameliorated."[4] This notion is close to the idea of primary-lesbian/bisexual-lesbian complementarity. However, Berzon does not explore unconscious dimensions of relating and is pessimistic about this basis for relating, noting its potential for mutual disappointment.

Phillip Blumstein and Pepper Schwartz's study includes interviews with five lesbian couples.[5] In this small sample, scant information is provided about partner choices. One couple is portrayed as a role-playing, butch-femme couple; however, the woman who is identified as femme influences her partner to give up her butch appearance and behavior—she does not seem to like gender-differentiated complementarity after all. One couple includes a previously married woman and a woman who was previously unclear about her sexual identity. One couple involves a previously married partner (who has some bisexual feelings still) and another who has been strictly lesbian.

In both of the remaining couples, the women were married when they met each other. One woman in each couple states that although she was married, the relationship never touched her deeply and that she clearly belongs with women. That is, one partner of each couple feels she was always lesbian but married anyway for other reasons. The other partner in one of these couples returned to men after the lesbian couple broke up, suggesting her underlying bisexuality. No further information is given about the remaining woman's sexuality. Although only one of Blumstein and Schwartz's couples absolutely fits a primary-lesbian/bisexual-lesbian pattern, three others approximate it. Even in the traditional role-playing couple, there is reason to question the nature of their connection.

Donna Tanner's study of lesbian couples is also a sociological rather than psychological study and likewise does not explore partner choice.[6] Nevertheless, her work does provide some clues about complementarity. Tanner notes that "some" (number unspecified) couples began their relationship when one partner was gay and one was straight. She categorizes couples into three groups: traditional-complementary (based on some degree of role-playing); flexible nurturing-caretaking (in which some economic dependence is involved); and negotiated-egalitarian (based on "equality and mutual independence"). In both the first and third types, Tanner notes that typically when they meet, one partner is gay whereas the other is not.

Because data on differences in sexual orientation between lesbian partners are so difficult to find, I made the survey of therapists who work with lesbian couples. A letter was sent to twelve therapists, explaining the nature of the study and seeking information through a questionnaire about how many of the couples they had seen in treatment during the preceding two years fit the pattern I was investigating, how many did not, and how many could not be specified. Of the twelve questionnaires mailed, eight (67 percent) were returned, but two therapists were unable to specify relevant data. The remaining six respondents provided the following information: of the seventy-four couples that could be categorized, forty-six (62 percent) fit the pattern, twenty-eight (38 percent) did not. Another twenty-three couples could not be categorized; the therapist did not know whether the individual partners were primary or bisexual lesbians.

This information tends to support the other suggestive evidence. Although the results of the survey likewise do not provide hard data, they do show that couples of this type are common. The survey raises other questions. Are such couples more or less commonly seen in treatment? If more, does such a difference create special problems for couples? If the couples are less commonly seen in treatment, do such differences create stability? Unfortunately, other studies of lesbian couples address complementarity only on the basis of whether a masculine-feminine dichotomy is involved—again, the stereotypical view of lesbian couples.

The Use of Small Differences

No clear-cut line divides primary lesbians from those who are bisexual. The quotations I chose in the previous chapter tend to reflect the ends of the continuum of lesbian orientations. I chose them because some women do find themselves on either end of such a continuum, and their experiences help to define and illuminate differences that are sometimes more subtle. Because more women probably find themselves (and their partners) somewhere closer to the middle of this continuum, I was particularly interested in how these women experienced or failed to experience differences.

Often, these women's perception of differences with their partners shifted. For example, within the same interview a woman might remark on how her interest in men was always greater than her partner's even though they were both involved with men earlier. She might later say, however, with some emphasis, "but she *was* involved with several men," that is, like herself. Then again, she might add, "I think these relationships were not very good" or "not very important."

None of the women doubted the category with which they identified, but two were unclear about their lovers, who seemed to have some characteristics of both groups. These women eventually came to a decision about whether they were different from their lovers on the basis of what they felt was an intuitive grasp of the lover's sexuality. That is, even though they knew something about the lover's process of coming out and whether or not she had been involved with men, they had to make their own distinctions about where the lover's real interests lay. Whether correct or not, these decisions reflect a sense of knowing about certain dimensions of the lover's psyche that may have never been discussed openly. They may even reflect unconscious wishes.

There is much room here for partners to make projections and subjective evaluations about each other, leaving open the question of how lovers use their own ideas (momentarily or in prolonged ways) to satisfy some unconscious purpose. Do women who are closer into the (hypothetical) mean between the extremes of such differences nevertheless mine this smaller difference for what it can offer? Is there still an impulse to find the kind of complementarity at issue here? I think partners often cooperate with these projections or unconscious uses of themselves because they, too, unconsciously experience the value of doing so for personal growth and for relational bonding. It is the playing within this imaginative area of the relationship, the "potential space" in D. W. Winnicott's thinking, wherein profoundly significant exchanges occur.

Invisible Cords: A Theory of Complementarity

The polarity between these different experiences of lesbianism—between those who are more exclusively lesbian and those who are more bisexual—constitutes a complementary potential between women who embody them. Their differences may be positively valued, negatively valued, or ambivalently valued, but the unconscious exchange in intimacy between partners will likely include these dimensions. Every direction taken in an individual life closes some routes of self-development while opening others. An experience one could have had, but never did, holds a continuing fascination to the psyche. It is a road not taken, and the psyche does not easily abandon interest in foreclosed experience. Through the intimacy of love and sexuality, one has another chance, a chance to pursue imaginatively, through merged experience and unconscious exchanges, unexplored routes.

The essence of this connection in lesbian relationships can be sketched briefly. In lesbian relationships of the kind I am describing, the differences between lovers become ties. Such ties, the invisible cords of a relationship, cross psychic experience, allowing each woman some access to her own uncharted routes. These ties exist in three primary dimensions of psychic experience: psychosexual development, the capacity to accept or incorporate the experience of difference, and gender development.

First, unconscious psychosexual interests, or each woman's different orientation to same-sex and opposite-sex relating, challenges and enriches the other. Second, each woman's sense of self as deviant or different, as normal or fitting in, and her ability to cope (or not cope) with difference are mediated through her lover's separate experience. Third, her gender-related experiences of self are matched against her partner's, often with an interest in expanding her sense of gendered self in both directions—both the masculine and the feminine—unlike the stereo-typical account.

In later chapters I will explore these three separate but interlocking dimensions of interpersonal exchange. The search for the meaning of this complementarity shifts between theoretical possibilities and inter-pretations of conversations between the women and myself. Much of what I am considering has to do with unconscious experience. As in clinical work, formulations about unconscious processes are difficult to verify and are open to different interpretations. The validity of interpretations, however, can be judged by their usefulness in illuminating what is otherwise mysterious, their internal theoretical consistency, their fruitfulness in leading to new insights, and repeated confirmations in other material.

For every couple the valence of any given dimension differs, sometimes considerably, from other couples, yet all three dimensions hover in the background of the relationship, carrying more or less of the developmental potential of that relationship. What determines the importance of a particular variable is the extent to which it intersects with pressing psychological concerns for individual women. Vitality in relationships is, I think, a direct function of the degree to which the complementarity created (imaginatively, sometimes) by differences such as these provides an arena for continuing individual development. These concerns are not the same for all couples. How these relational exchanges occur, how they are communicated unconsciously, and why we seek differences in relationships are the subjects of the next two chapters.

The Psychological
Function of
Relationships

4

Romantic and sexual attraction between two people often defies logic and circumstance. We all know that everyone is somehow more suited or more attracted to some people than to others, but we are usually at a loss to explain why. We think of someone having a "type" to whom she or he is attracted, but this type may be defined by physique, personality or temperment, ethnic features, or vocation or avocation. While we can often discern a roughly drawn picture of someone's romantic interests, we do not necessarily know why this pattern holds or, even more curiously, why it sometimes does not. When a friend or relative chooses a partner who seems unsuitable, we shake our heads at the impossibility of explaining love. We cannot predict who will fall in love with whom. Sometimes we are even surprised by ourselves.

The idea of complementarity attempts to address this mystery. It refers to the often-inexplicable fit between two partners, that which makes them feel well-suited to each other even beyond their own comprehension. To complement something is to complete it, to fill it up, to make it perfect or whole. This immediately recalls Aristophanes' tale in Plato's *Symposium*, in which love is explained as the search for the lost half of oneself. Even if there is an intuitive truth to this myth, many questions remain. What makes someone the "other half" (or, as some say, "better half") of another? How is it that we recognize that potential in another? In this chapter I will explore the nature of complementarity in intimate relationships and suggest at least some pieces of the puzzle.

Psychoanalytic Theory and Complementarity

The issues of love and the choice of love objects are remarkably unexplored in psychoanalytic theory. In fact, psychoanalysis explores complementarity in relationships largely through the transference-countertransference relationship in the therapeutic setting. Analytic theory argues that the fit between lovers can be traced to some aspect of the early relationship with parents. As Freud notes, "love consists of new editions of old traces and . . . it repeats infantile reactions. . . . [T]his is the essential character of every love. There is no love that does not reproduce infantile prototypes."[1]

In her analysis of love relationships, Ethel Person extends Freud's insight. New lovers draw upon all lost loves. "Freud's great insight into love was to demonstrate the continuity, despite appearances to the contrary, of the lover's emotional life, and to flesh out the Platonic insight that the union in love is really a reunion. . . . The enormous power the beloved seems to exert on the lover can in part be explained by the love object having been invested with the mystique of all the lost objects from the past. . . . In love the lover regains his lost omnipotence, takes total possession of the beloved and achieves Oedipal victory." Not only lost loves are found in the beloved, however. One also finds again the lost self, or part of the self: "one's love object may also embody some buried aspiration of the self."[2] Thus in psychoanalytic theory, Aristophanes' fable holds as well. The elements of reunion are interwoven and sometimes difficult to distinguish. Others are loved because they have been invested with qualities of one's own internal, unconscious self and object images. Even from the beginning of a relationship, the distinction between self and other is never absolute.

The psychoanalytic concept of projective identification, discussed more fully in the next chapter, suggests how this investment of the self in others takes place. Parts of the self (e.g., feelings, desires or impulses, internal objects, or object relationships) are projected onto the other, who, through identification, comes to hold or express that part of the self and seems to embody it. The mutuality of this process between lovers bonds them. Person discusses the ways these unconscious exchanges enrich the loving relationship: "In idyllic love, the lovers achieve an oscillating balance between giving and receiving, active and passive roles, pleasing and being pleased, enacting the role now of the child, now of the parent. In moving back and forth between these two roles, the lover experiences the vital interests of the beloved as his own, and he values her pleasure and happiness as much as his own.

His identification with her is so complete that she assumes an importance commensurate with his own."[3] Through identification with each other, and with what the other has come to embody of the self, lovers find fulfillment.

The psychoanalytic view of the relationship between therapist and client rests upon the same complementarity as well—a search for new experiences with self and other, ultimately arising out of early object relationships. About transference, Freud points out that "every human being has acquired, by the combined operation of inherent disposition and of external influences in childhood, a special individuality in the exercise of his capacity to love. . . . As we should expect, this accumulation of libido will be attached to prototypes, bound up with one of the cliches already established in the mind of the person concerned, or, to put it another way, the patient will weave the figure of the physician into one of the 'series' already constructed in his mind."[4]

The interplay in intimate relationships is a form of transference, like that of a therapeutic relationship. The oedipal relationship (the child-parent "love affair") is transferred onto a new person who seems to resemble (perhaps only unconsciously) the old one. The lover has attributes of the now-internalized parent. It is important to remember, however, that the internal object image itself may bear little resemblance to the actual parent.

The psyche selects and transforms perceptions of the parent in the internalization process so that the internal object is likely to be only an aspect (which was important in some way) of the parent. Other aspects are ignored or transformed in other ways, or they become internalized as other object images. Internal parent images may be almost totally unlike the parent—a negation of the actual parent, an idealization of the parent, or a creation of a longed-for parent that barely resembles actuality. Further, parental images may also include elements of both mother and father.

Because there are multiple internalized parent figures (different aspects of the parents are never fully integrated), there are also different self-images. Each parent-image has an accompanying image of the self in relationship to it, and each of these internalized relationships has a distinct emotional tone, often intense and largely unconscious. For example, in one's inner world there may be a nurturing parent related to a well-loved, secure self, but there may also be a demanding, critical parent in perpetual struggle with a defiant yet anxious self.

These internal, affectively charged relationships of self and other are dynamic structures, the fundamental structures of the psyche, according to object-relations theory.[5] They not only serve as passive templates for interpreting one's experiences in the world, but they also generate intrapsychic experience reflected in interpersonal encounters. For example, in one's most intimate relationship one may continually recreate encounters that mirror the struggle between a critical other and a defiant, anxious self—a way of externalizing and coping with what is essentially an internal experience. One might also reverse the roles, embodying the other in one's own actions. These are the psyche's ways of creating, organizing, and making sense of the external world.

The internal world is obviously complicated, and adults draw upon this complexity in making choices of lovers. As Martin Bergmann notes, the new object must evoke the old, but not too closely: "it must not awaken incestuous guilt." The lover wishes to remain unaware of the sources of a new love's attraction. People seek to recreate unconscious relationships with different internalized others ("each object of infancy demands its own re-finding") at different times in their lives or within one relationship.[6]

To complicate matters further, the lover also projects parts of her or his self-image as well as parental images onto the beloved in a way that both attracts and binds the couple. The loved one may need to reflect an integration of different images of one's self. For example, Bergmann explains, "Bisexuality is a universal human endowment, but individuals differ in the strength of their respective masculine and feminine components, and they seek in the partner a corresponding mixture of the two components." At the same time, projection may be used to evade the ambiguity and tension of cross-gender identifications. In heterosexual coupling, "feminine wishes in the man and masculine wishes in the woman are projected onto the partner, enhancing one's own gender identity and therefore the boundaries of the self."[7]

Several more theoretical examples from analytic literature address this projection and find again the unconscious dimensions of the self. Disowned attributes of the self draw one "like a magnet. A man may be attracted to a very narcissistic woman because the narcissism which his conscious idealization forces him to renounce continues to pull him unconsciously. A woman may be drawn to a man for the boyish qualities she herself possessed before she had to abandon them for 'girl's' behavior."[8] In heterosexual relationships, the man and woman use each other to amplify gender identity. "He [the lover] also projects onto her [the beloved] his own femininity and his own wishes and then tries to live up to her imagined expectations of him. A kind of identification is thereby effected through which he is partly in love with himself as he sees himself reflected in his conception of her."[9]

These analyses of masculine and feminine projections point to what the psychoanalyst Joyce McDougall describes as "one of the greatest narcissistic wounds of childhood . . . our ineluctable monosexuality."[10] Reality requires the child to accept that he or she cannot be both sexes, but this acceptance is traumatic. It leaves each of us with the consequent "problem of what to do with our psychic bisexuality."

Typically, psychoanalytic writers confuse or equate bisexuality (interest in lovers of either sex) with gender identifications (the sense of being masculine or feminine). These writers are generally concerned with cross-gender identity rather than sexual orientation when they refer to bisexuality as a factor in unconscious relating or choosing a lover. Both bisexuality and bi-gender identifications play a vital role in conscious and unconscious object choice for homosexual and heterosexual lovers alike. In various ways, everyone seeks resolution of these conflicts through the intimacy of love relationships. The lover who expresses that part of oneself that lacks conscious expression is a desired Other.

Clearly, this complexity of expectations may not be so easy to satisfy in reality. The psyche often becomes creative, turning the beloved into the desired one. The new loved one may seem to have certain attributes, largely because the lover has endowed him or her with these via projection. John Money draws an analogy between the lover and the Rorschach inkblot. With this metaphor he captures the subjectively defined nature of love partners. "In many instances, a person does not fall in love with a partner, per se, but with a partner as a Rorschach love-blot. That is to say, the person projects onto the partner an idealized and highly idiosyncratic image that diverges from the image of that partner as perceived by other people."[11]

The idea of the lover as a "love-blot" helps to explain the unconscious processes at work in the choice of a partner who surprises those outside of the relationship. The lover sees something in the beloved that no one else sees, perhaps a part of the lover's self (that is, an internal image in the lover's psyche) as much as part of the beloved. What the beloved has to offer is a uniquely suited aptitude for holding this projection.

Money goes further. " 'Pair-bonding' is a growth experience, like a religious one, as each partner "accedes to being made over in the image of the other, at least to some degree."[12] Some kind of "complementary cues and collusive signals" are probably necessary ahead of time, cues that indicate a willingness for this exchange. Long-term relationships are created when there is sufficient mutuality in this process. This reciprocity of fit is most important, he argues. Complementarity is not determined by principles of either sameness or difference.

A long-lasting reciprocal love-match between two partners is one in which there is reciprocally a very close love-blot match. That means there is a very close fit between the actuality of each partner and the love-blot image projected onto him or her by the other partner, and this is a two-way fit. For this high degree of fit to take place, it is irrelevant whether the two partners are replicas or polar opposites of one another in temperament, interests, achievements, or whatever. What counts is that they fulfill in each the other's ideal in imagery and expectancy, even though neither may be able to spell out this expectancy in words. Over the years, what also counts is that change of imagery and expectancy, if it takes place, is mutual and not one-sided.[13]

Most psychoanalytic studies focus primarily on neurotic or otherwise pathological variations of the bonds of love, implicitly devaluing passion for its irrational aspects.[14] As Money suggests, however, love is also transformative. It is an urge to expand the self, even an impulse toward healing wounds to the self. Love can be compared to religious or mystical experiences that transform the self. Like them, love involves merger, a crossing of boundaries between self and other. This is not a a permanent creation of a fused state, but a transient partaking of it that is both healing and expansive. Through immersion in an Other, whether a person or an experience such as art or religion, "the sense of self is continuously enriched."[15]

Ethel Person likewise points to the transforming character of love through merger. "Having transcended the boundaries of the self by identifying with the Other, the lover is empowered beyond the usual, and no longer bound by old patterns, habits, and other rigidities of character. This is one of the reasons that falling in love and achieving mutual love are often accompanied by spurts of energy, growth, and change and by a sense of richness and abundance."[16]

In a love match, then, each partner already partly embodies and each also begins to take on some greater part of a longed-for image the other holds. To be successful, the relationship must allow both parties to find such fulfillment in the other and then shift over time as each partner's internal world shifts. The relationship is an arena for the delicate interplay of fulfillment, disappointments, and accommodations. The disappointments and accommodations become catalysts for internal changes that are eventually returned to the interpersonal arena, seeking fulfillment on new terms. Conceiving of love relationships in this way begins to indicate the importance of complementarity for relationships and the importance of relationships for adult development.

Complementarity, Relationships, and Adult Development

What do we need from a concept of complementarity? Clearly, some way to understand why individuals are drawn to particular others, male or female. An even more basic question concerns why anyone invites intimacy with a relative stranger, allowing an unpredictable other, an apparently unknown entity, to enter one's deepest psychic and emotional life. Intimacy gives access to one's essential vulnerability in ways that are inevitably filled with risk. What need or desire impels individuals to take such risks, often again and again in spite of painful experience and failed hopes?

Object-relations theory answers this question by positing that the nature of the human psyche is inherently object-seeking, not pleasure-seeking as Freud proposed.[17] The need for relatedness to others is built into the organism. Growth and development take place only in the context of object-relating. Some feminist psychoanalytic writers suggest that this is more true for women than for men.[18] Pathological consequences follow the failure, or absence, of the object. Indeed, in this case relating to the absence of the object defines development.[19]

It is not simply the object that is important, but the relationship between self and object. Just as the psyche originally becomes stable through internalizing relationships, the link between self and other continues to be the arena for development in adult years. Thinking of relationships as a developmental arena is the abstraction D. W. Winnicott conceived of as "potential space": "It is useful, then, to think of a third area of human living, one neither inside the individual nor outside in the world of shared reality. This intermediate living can be thought of as occupying a potential space, negating the idea of space and separation."[20]

Potential space is a hypothetical area created between the self and the other, the space of their relatedness. Imaginative elaborations on reality, or "playing" as Winnicott calls it, occur as the boundary between "me" and "not-me" is transcended. Here, unconscious illusion exists without the interference of reality, yet paradoxically it does not deny reality either. This psychic dimension is important in adult relating that transcends the constraints of reality, especially that of separateness: "The potential space is thus the place where meaningful communication takes place. It is the common ground in affectionate relationships. . . . Here communication comes about through 'mutuality in experience' or the overlap of potential spaces."[21] The link between self and other, then, is the area for expansion of the self—the means, perhaps the primary means, for growth and development to occur.

Here one can imaginatively take on (and finally take in) new dimensions of external reality. The child's earliest experiences of separation out of merger with the mother occur in that potential space in which separateness is both accepted and negated.[22] The child and the adult alike work out the various losses, separations, new additions, and attachments in the inner world through the arena of potential space in which the distinctions between inner and outer reality are eclipsed.

Andre Green, like Winnicott, notes that "in the phrase 'object relation' the word 'relation' is the more important one. . . . In other words, the study of relations is that of the links rather than that of the terms united by them."[23] He explores the complementary interplay between self and other as the source of psychic development, and his thoughts about the intrapsychic-interpersonal dimension of analytic treatment also apply to intimate relationships. As Green explains it, in the analytic setting the process between patient and analyst creates a "double" of the other in each—the "analytic object."

> The patient's communication—different from what he lives and feels—is situated in the transitional space between him and us, in the same way our interpretation is carried by communication. . . . Thus even when the work of analysis compels the analyst to make great efforts, which lead him to form a picture in his mind of the patient's mental functioning, he supplies what is missing in the patient. I have said that he replaced the part which is missing . . . through observing homologous processes in himself. *But the real analytic object is neither on the patient's side nor on the analyst's, but in the meeting of these two communications in the potential space which lies between them.* . . . If we consider that each party present, the patient and the analyst, is composed of the union of two parts (what they live and what they communicate), one of which is the double of the other . . . one can see that the analytic object is formed of two doubles, one belonging to the patient and the other to the analyst. . . . For, in order to have a formation of an analytic object, an essential condition is the establishment of homologous and complementary relations between the patient and the analyst. . . . From this point of view the analyst does not only unveil a hidden meaning. He constructs a meaning which has never been created before the analytic relationship began.[24]

Here Green finds the original meaning of the word *symbolic*. A symbol is "an object cut in two constituting a sign of recognition when those who carry it can assemble the two pieces."[25] His concept of the analytic experience can be extended to ordinary relating, to what may exist only within relationship. Intimate relationships parallel analytic ones and create a new space that contains meanings that did not exist before. New or previously undeveloped parts of the self come into being through these new meanings. When lovers come together, they each seem to carry a piece of the other, pieces that can now be joined through intimacy. This is the symbolic meaning of a relationship.

Relationship is an imaginative extension of self into other and other into self, creating a double of each individual. There is the "you" I both apprehend and create, the "you" to whom I relate, who is different from the "you" you experience yourself to be. There is the "me" you apprehend, create, and relate to, who is different from the me I know. I can partake of this me through you, and vice-versa. It is one of the meanings of the idea that through relationship with an other, one finds oneself. This other you and other me may contain what has been lost to each of us about ourselves, what is unconscious or even inchoate.

Of course, this different me may not be one to whom I can relate. It may contain perceptions of me that I resist experiencing. It may seem not to be me at all, but simply more of you, too entirely a product of your own projection of self. On the other hand, your projections of yourself onto this me may contain elements with which I can identify or wish to incorporate. These enrich my sense of self. They in turn affect the you I perceive and send out to you. I can enter this intermediate zone of the relationship in which I am both myself and some of you, which allows me to find even more of myself. I can give you some unknown part of myself and discover what it is like. You may, in turn, alter and send back a new me. These exchanges constitute the unconscious play of relationship in which reality and illusion comingle.

Complementarity as Unconscious Knowledge and Desire

It is now more clear how complementarity is a necessary concept. One's willingness to partake of these exchanges occurs only where there is some sense of fit. This relational play must take place with an other whose projections will suit and will to some extent be welcomed, or at least tolerated. Thus complementarity is determined by some unconscious perception of prior familiarity, an unconscious grasp of the fit between the other and one's own internal objects. This is the sense, often experienced by lovers in an intense new romance, of having always known the other person.

Equally important, complementarity promises enrichment in a direction that is meaningful to the self. When Money writes of the beloved's willingness to be made over according to the image of the lover, he means that the loved person gives over to this process not only to create a bond with the lover, but also because the process resonates at a deep level with some part of her or his own psyche. She or he is responding to an invitation for a new part of the self to make its appearance. Thus it is never a matter of being molded solely by the lover's desires, but always a correspondence of desire, however unconscious, to discover this aspect of the self.

We use relationships to find in ourselves what we cannot find alone. Without relationships that touch the psyche in such meaningful ways, we would continue to live in ignorance of much of who we are. Fairy tales express this experience through stories that describe a sleeping beauty awakened by a kiss. In relationships, the dormant or uncreated self responds to such contact, which promises to bring it to life. We are capable of this kind of knowledge through projective identification, the psychoanalytic version of unconscious communication.

Unconscious Conversations

5 How do we sometimes know things about another person without really knowing that person? Intuition and empathy are means of knowing that are not encompassed by the usual, conscious observation and perception processes. Likewise, sometimes we deny knowing something about another that our behavior suggests we do know. For example, a woman becomes involved again and again with partners who are critical and rejecting yet says each time that she thought the new lover was different. She is shocked and upset to discover that she has chosen yet another impossible lover. Clearly, people know things about each other that are excluded from their conscious awareness. This chapter will explore the ways that unconscious communication plays a part in the mystery of attraction and intimate bonding.

The example of the woman who, to her dismay, keeps choosing the same kind of partner suggests two different processes at work. Perhaps she has unconscious knowledge that is categorically different from what she consciously thinks. That is, she unconsciously detects the negative aspect of the lover even while consciously she believes a romance with great potential is underway. Another possibility is that she evokes a critical, rejecting aspect in every lover she chooses. What starts off as a happy and promising love affair gradually deteriorates into an unhappy repetition of former affairs. Does this woman somehow know her prospective lover will reject her, or does she manage to bring this about herself? The mechanism of projective identification is a way to explain both possibility.

How anyone apprehends the psychological state of another is a basic question. Psychoanalytic thinking holds that people have the capacity to partake of complex communicative processes on an unconscious level, usually experienced in treatment as transference and countertransference: "the basic assumption is that the analyst's unconscious understands that of his patient."[1] Concepts of empathy and projective identification are used to explain this interpersonal capacity. Sigmund Freud described empathy as an outcome of identification: "A path leads from identification by way of imitation to empathy."[2] Many writers think of empathy as a form of identification, sometimes as "trial identification" or "transient identification."[3] The role of projection and introjection as the essential connective mechanisms for forming these empathic identifications is emphasized by object-relations theorists.[4] Some psychoanalytic theorists view projective identification as the fundamental basis of all relating.[5] In this chapter I hope to show how the concept of projective identification most aptly captures the way that individuals both apprehend and make use of another's subjectivity, especially at unconscious levels.

The term *projective identification* refers to an integration of projection with identification process. In the combined unconscious transaction one person projects an aspect of her or his mental functioning—thoughts, feelings, and impulses—onto another and thereby comes to identify with that person. Introjective identification is the process in reverse, involving an unconscious introjection of an aspect of another person and a subsequent identification. These processes generate a powerful unconscious bond between two people, as one holds or carries a part of the other, psychologically speaking.

Projective and introjective identifications are the psyche's means of communicating at unconscious levels. They allow people to know themselves and each other, even when conscious self-image is at odds with this knowledge. Because the full circle of both projection and introjection is generally involved in either process, it is simplest to use only one term even though both are occurring. Projective identification is a difficult concept to employ, however, because different analytic writers use it in different ways. Each meaning and use of the term contributes to a full appreciation of a highly complex but fundamental psychic process.

How Projective Identification Works

Projective identification may function defensively as a way of getting rid of unacceptable attributes or feelings that are causing tension and inner conflict. When another person stands for or embodies that part of the self in the projector's mind, the projector no longer experiences the thought or feeling as her or his own. Freedom from unwanted thoughts and feelings, relief from tension, or a false sense of resolution may be achieved in this way. For example, if a man has ambivalent feelings about his son, he may project the negative side of this ambivalence onto his wife. To him, the wife now seems more hostile to the child than he, and he becomes protective. His own unconscious hostility toward his son is too disturbing for him to tolerate and come to terms with, so it is imaginatively ejected onto his wife. The father's positive feelings for the child are heightened then, especially as he becomes more protective.

The father's hostile feelings toward the child may arise from projective identification. Suppose the father unconsciously has a negative view of maleness (perhaps a feeling that men are lacking in some way that women are not). The son becomes the target of the father's projection of this unconscious negative assessment, and the father is again somewhat relieved of his own internal tension. It is the son who is lacking, not himself, and the wife who sees him as inferior. Now the father's inner conflicts are played out between the boy and his mother. He can experience the other side of these feelings and appreciate his son's maleness while protecting him from the imagined hostility of the wife.

This example expresses one aspect of projective identification. One projects unacceptable feelings or impulses onto another while identifying that part of the self with the other. The other becomes an unconscious extension of the self and therefore important to the self. A bond is generated between the two that will give the other special significance as long as the projection holds. The self is in effect saying to the other, "You are this part of me, and I need to maintain my connection with you."

A second level of complication is added by the interaction between the man and his wife. She may come to resent her husband's protectiveness toward their son. It makes her feel as if she is a threat to him. She also may envy the special consideration the son evokes from her husband while she is treated quite differently. She begins, in fact, to feel hostility toward her son. Now she has begun to identify with her husband's projection onto her. As a consequence of the family's interactions, she is hostile to the son and must figure out how to deal with these feelings.

Some psychoanalytic writers think of projective identification as the process described first in this example. The projector identifies with the recipient of the projection, forming the bond of projective identification. The original conception of the process was Melanie Klein's. Her work suggests that identification may occur on the subject's (the self's) part without involvement necessary on the object's (the other's) part. For Klein, projective identification is a mechanism by which the object becomes a part of the self.[6]

Klein was intensely concerned with introjection and projection, as well as splitting, in early development, believing these to be the basic ways infants form connections with other people (projection) and build intrapsychic structure through continually modifying their internal world of inner objects (introjection).[7] Children commonly project their difficult emotions onto someone else, often the mother. They also introject aspects of the mother for greater sense of security. A continual process of exchange thus takes place between internal and external reality. Too much projection leaves one feeling depleted and needing to control the other who carries so much of the self, however. Too much introjection leaves one feeling invaded. New anxieties are then generated by these processes: fear of being controlled by the other or of losing control.

However, projection does not always involve unacceptable or difficult impulses. It is not always defensive, nor is it necessarily depleting. Good feelings and desires are also projected, making one more desirous of intimacy. Conversely, when the other is felt to be good, the psyche partakes of this goodness through introjection. In this way the complementary processes of projection and introjection are how the internal world is built up and object relations internalized. Thus projection and introjection are not necessarily defensive processes at all, but rather intrinsic means of psychic development. Fragmented or split-off parts of the self and its related objects are continuously projected and introjected until they gradually become more coherent and whole.

Writers have used other terms for the same mechanism. Anna Freud called it "altruistic surrender." As she explained, unacceptable impulses are projected onto another person with whom one comes to identify. The other person may then be championed in carrying out these impulses. Freud describes a young woman who projected her sexual and narcissistic desires onto another woman, then felt bonded with this woman. With no concern for her own happiness she could then encourage the other woman to date and wear beautiful clothes. This mechanism, Freud wrote, enables "us to form valuable positive attachments and so to consolidate our relations with one another."[8]

Is there a distinction to be made between projection and projective identification? Some analytic writers say no, arguing that identification always involves projection (and introjection), and projection always involves some measure of identifying with the object.[9] "When we start with the projection it is necessary that there be some process of identification or internalization in general, or else we can never be aware of the projection. That is, what is projected would be lost like a satellite rocketed out of the gravitational pull of the earth. Eventually all contact with the satellite will be lost."[10]

Others disagree, however. They distinguish projection from projective identification according to whether or not an "interpersonal press" is exerted between the projector and the recipient, so that the recipient comes to identify with the projection as well.[11] In the example given previously, when the mother experiences hostility toward the son, she is identifying with the projection. The father's behavior toward her and the son constitutes the interpersonal press that induces her identification with his projection, completing the link of projective identification between them. This process has also been likened to "evocation of a proxy." The subject induces the object to identify with the projection and thus to carry out the subject's disowned impulses: "a thing, a person, or an image, created and invoked to play a role in the service of the self."[12] This phenomenon is universal and especially common between couples. For example, to lessen the burden of her own anger, a woman may unconsciously promote her partner's anger toward someone with whom the woman is angry.

When projective identification is used defensively, to get rid of unacceptable feelings or impulses, it may still have a purpose beyond simple relief of tension. The person who projects engages the other's participation in some way so that the other person must deal with the difficult feelings. If the other person gradually processes the feelings, she or he has indicated a way to tolerate and perhaps even transform them. In this way difficult feelings may become more acceptable.

The one who projects may be able to internalize the other's dealing with these feelings, bringing the process full circle. What was originally projected may now be reintrojected and reowned. In this way, the psyche attempts to come to terms (through a circuitous route) with something heretofore impossible to manage. Again returning to the preceding example, when the father projects his negative feelings onto his wife and son, he also pays attention to how they cope with these feelings. If they handle them better than he has, he himself may become more at ease with his feelings. His need for defensive projection then diminishes.

The content of projections may be feelings, thoughts, or impulses. It may be of another order entirely. A person may project aspects of internalized object relationships, either the self or the object aspect, onto another and engage the other to act out the relationship between them. In the example of the woman who continues to find critical and rejecting partners, the recurrence could be understood as evidence that the woman projects onto her partners her own internalized critical love object (an aspect of one of the parents, for example) and then manages to evoke expression of the object in each new lover. In this way she recreates once again an old relationship to which she is still bound unconsciously.

These descriptions refer to one-way complementarity, where one party is drawn into the inner world of the other's relationships. The ideal complementarity described in the last chapter is achieved when lovers are able to work this exchange both ways, more positively imbued. A mutuality of projective and introjective identification allows each to find again a world of lost others and parts of the self and perhaps see how these identifications are reworked by the other so that they may be transformed.

Progressive and Regressive Aspects of Projective Identification

Disagreements over the distinction between empathy and projective identification have been created by using nonequivalent definitions of projective identification. Those who limit it to a defensive or pathological process distinguish it sharply from empathy.[13] In this view, projective identification is simply a way to disown and evade unwanted parts of the psyche. Whatever is difficult to deal with is ejected from the psyche in fantasy, so the process of development is derailed. The projector must maintain the fantasy state and can no longer negotiate reality. This is only one of Klein's conceptions of the process. She and later object-relations theorists understood projective identification to be a much richer and more vital mechanism than its defensive uses suggest.

Again, some theorists see projective identification as fundamental to all human relating, and others view it as a vital means of growth and development as well as a defensive maneuver. Thomas Ogden points to the broad range of functions that projective identification may serve:

As a defense, projective identification serves to create a sense of psychological distance from unwanted, often frightening aspects of the self. As a mode of communication, projective identification is a process by which feelings congruent with one's own are induced in another person, thereby creating a sense of being understood by or "at one with" the other person. As a type of object relations, projective identification constitutes a way of being with and relating to a partially separate object. Finally as a pathway for psychological change, projective identification is a process by which feelings like those that one is struggling with are psychologically processed by another person and made available for reinternalization in an altered form.[14]

Others who also stress that projective identification is both a defense and "a way of relating to objects," that it is part of mature as well as defensive relating, think of these processes as intrinsic to intrapsychic growth and development. For example, "projecting one's inner psychic contents into external objects and then perceiving the response of these external objects and introjecting this response on a new level of integration is the way in which the human organism grows psychically, nurtured by his environment."[15]

It is ironic that projective identification has so often been cast in a pathological light because the process of psychotherapy relies upon the potential for this kind of interpersonal exchange. Andre Green's account of the intricacies of unconscious communication in the analytic relationship (chapter 4) describes this process most fully. An analytic understanding of interpersonal processes has evolved slowly, often against resistance in the psychoanalytic movement. Countertransference, for example, was thought of first as an entirely neurotic response on the part of the analyst. As long as it was interpreted this way, analysts tended to avoid writing about their own internal processes during analytic sessions, treating them as problems to be resolved privately.[16] A gradual shift in psychoanalysis away from a strictly intrapsychic view of development (and, as far as possible, even of treatment) toward an interpersonal, interactive view has been under way in the last decades and is becoming dominant.[17]

The therapeutic relationship has received more scrutiny and has been analyzed more thoroughly than other kinds of relationships. This is not surprising; analysts have more immediate access to this relationship than to others. Even the love relationships of the analysand are once-removed and are often known best through their vicarious manifestations in the therapeutic relationship. Only in analyses of the therapeutic relationship is a detailed look at both sides of a relationship possible. In both love relationships and therapeutic ones, the important mechanism of linkage between the unconscious of each partner, that which creates and helps sustain the bond between the two, is a form of identification (introjective or projective).

The problem is that clinical perspectives are skewed toward developmental difficulties, and analysts often forget that their view is not a whole one. Projective identifications experienced in this setting occur in all of their functions, but are probably tilted toward defensive manifestations. Consequently, although almost all conceptions of projective identification include recognition of its powerful role in growth and development, the majority of analytic writings focuses on its pathological aspect. This skewed account is especially true in clinical reports of intimate relationships.[18] Nevertheless, these explorations also suggest that partners have some unconscious means of knowing the other's potential for carrying their own projections and that this potential is a fundamental determinant of attraction between people.

Projective Identification in Intimate Relationships

Sigmund Freud noted that projections require some basis in reality. The individual does not make projections "into the sky, so to speak," but is guided by "knowledge of the unconscious."[19] Klein was probably the first to argue that projective identification determines object choice in love relationships, that the search for the lost ideal self and lost objects gives impetus to projective identifications, which then pave the way for falling in love with someone new. She points out that some common ground with the object of the projection appears to be necessary, although a sense of commonality is created simultaneously with the projection process.[20]

The theoretical work on marital relationships developed by the Tavistock Clinic in London, especially during the 1960s, drew upon British psychoanalytic theory (object-relations theory). It examined how projective identification provides a marital bond. The partners of a couple relationship form "the two halves of a whole ... the parts of one partner's personality that he does not recognize are projected onto the other partner, who acts them out and expresses them."[21] For example, a clinical account in the literature from the Tavistock work describes a wife who carries the husband's harsh superego and depression, while the husband carries the role of the wife's rejecting mother. Even here, however, this process is understood as one of growth as well as defense. "The projected part of oneself can appear less destructive and frightening when it is experienced in someone else. Consequently, projection facilitates one's acceptance of his feared attributes."[22]

This mechanism is a form of "unconscious collusion" in a relationship. Through projective identification, one partner lives out some part of the other's reality, often from a pathological perspective, but the collusive interaction may nevertheless be beneficial and have a positive effect on both partners. The potential of a relationship to serve this function may even determine object choice, with an underlying urge toward growth and health. "Projective identification often forms the basis of a kind of unconscious wisdom in choosing a marital partner. It reflects the marital partners' efforts to make contact with the unrecognized, disowned characteristics that they have projected onto each other."[23]

More recently, Polly Crisp has also argued that complementarity is both discovered and created through projective identification. Each partner hopes to find something of herself or himself in the other, especially unconscious or disowned parts of the self. Projections may involve splitting along dimensions of the good and bad self or active and passive elements. Such complementarity may be a basis for either oppositional conflict or a state of balance, with positive consequences.

Raising questions about how objects are chosen as recipients for projection, Crisp points out that it is easier to identify projectively with someone who is actually complementary to oneself. For example, the wife projects her feelings of anger onto her husband, who in reality has difficulty controlling his temper. She posits several variables that may determine a fit. The recipient may be more receptive to projections as a consequence of "ego-boundary weakness or sensitivity." Perhaps the "projector 'tunes in' to the recipient's weakness in a specific area and projectively identifies into this area of the recipient."[24]

When one tunes into another's potential for projective identification, a kind of complementarity is under negotiation. An interactive balance is being sought in particularly meaningful areas. For this complementarity to hold, the partners must have some security in their own limits. As Crisp says, the ability to take in or contain projective identification requires a stable ego boundary. At the same time, boundaries must not be too rigid, an ability to relax them is also necessary. Such fluidity "may be indicative of underlying vulnerability or pathology, or of a form of mature sensitivity."[25] Crisp's discussion of this process recalls the dynamics of merger, both its power for enhancing the self and its risk of diminishing the self.

The emphasis in Crisp's work is again on pathological possibilities for such unconscious exchanges, although she recognizes their creative potential and their role in maintaining "a positive state of balance" in relating. This failure to explore the role of complementary projective and introjective mechanisms as a progressive vehicle in relationships, rather than a regressive or defensive one, is found throughout the literature. All of the major theorists of projective identification note its universal use and even its transformative capacities, yet by far the bulk of their work is devoted to how it is employed in pathological ways. In fact, the presence of projective identification is often regarded as evidence of disturbed functioning.

Perhaps this emphasis is understandable because excessive (however one may come to that determination) and pathological manifestations draw more attention to themselves. However, one of my intentions is to deepen the analysis of projective and introjective identifications in mature relating. Although the psychoanalytic conceptualization of object choice and complementarity through projection and introjection has a long history, it lacks a more complete understanding of the way projective exchanges work in positive ways, how they attract and hold partners to each other in ways that promote growth and development.

Theorists invariably point out the transformative capacity of projective identification, yet the idea has been put to little use in thinking about what Ethel Person calls "good love."[26] The concept is ripe with possibilities for further exploration. It is particularly rich in its power to understand the bond between primary and bisexual lesbians who may engage in multiple levels of such unconscious exchanges. One of the women I interviewed spontaneously expressed this process. Janine said that the interplay around differences in her relationship with Karen interests her because "It's a way of claiming something without absolutely having to be it." Her description expresses a progressive view of projective identification. The second part of this book is devoted to detailing such interpersonal exchanges in lesbian relationships.

Two | Invisible Cords: Complementarity

Psychosexual Interests: Past, Present, and Future

6 We return now to the question of complementarity in lesbian relationships with more pieces of the puzzle in place. Understanding the interplay between internal and external experience as lesbian identity illuminates differences between primary and bisexual lesbians. Projective identification explains how the sometimes-mystifying complementarity found in intimate relationships relies upon a largely unconscious process. Three major areas of difference between primary and bisexual lovers create attractions and serve as bonds.

First, differences in lesbian orientation reflect intrapsychic differences. The basic orientation of primary lesbians is toward women; men as potential choices are much further in the background, relatively undeveloped or repressed possibilities. Both men and women may be of erotic interest for bisexual lesbians, but the balance has tipped toward women as partners. Why the balance has shifted in this direction is idiosyncratic. One explanation does not suffice, and a combination of intrapsychic and situational circumstances in later life determines the outcome.

Second, primary and bisexual lesbians may feel the influence of social experience interacting with developing identity in different ways. A sense of self as more "different" or more "normal" is at issue. Primary lesbians know themselves to be different from the dominant culture and may have suffered to some degree from the stigma of deviance. Bisexual lesbians have a foothold in both worlds and have experienced both "normal" heterosexuality and "deviancy."

Third, the question arises of differences in gender identity. This is not a matter of core gender identity, that is, whether or not a woman is troubled about her gender; it refers instead to her socially developed sense of self as masculine, feminine, or androgynous. Thus it is a largely conscious sense of her individuality in cultural terms. Differences encompass the stereotypes of butch and femme but may also be expressed in much broader and less stereotyped ways.

These differences constitute a potential basis for complementarity in relationships between women who embody them. The other's potential as a recipient for certain kinds of projections is a source of attraction, while the identification engendered thereby serves as a bond. When the process is two-sided, and the partners engage in projective interplay, complementarity exists.

Psychosexual Exchanges

The bond between the primary lesbian and the bisexual lesbian allows each to stand in oblique relationship to her own potential bisexuality or primary lesbianism, respectively. The possibility exists for exchange of unconscious experience in early resolutions of oedipal love (that love affair between child and parent). For example, a woman whose experience has been primarily lesbian might project her own closed-off, heterosexual oedipal experience onto her more bisexually oriented lover. However she may feel about her lover's sexual interest in men, she may recognize in it some sense of her own lost experience.

She does not wish to live out this experience, to become heterosexual, but she has unconscious knowledge of her own lost experience, in effect a lost part of herself. She may be able to find this experience more happily in her partner. Paradoxically, she experiences an unconscious reunion with her own bisexuality within a lesbian relationship. Again, this brings her a fuller experience of herself rather than a desire to be with men. Her fundamental choice (an intrapsychic construct that may be relatively fixed) continues to be with women. Paula, who had never been involved with a man, discussed how relationships with bisexual lesbians had affected her feelings of alienation from men.

> I feel like it's . . . educated me. I've questioned women who've been with men, you know—"So what is it like? Why did you do it? What did you get from it? How is sex different?" Now I'd say that I choose women much less out of negative reasons like fear of men. Now I just think that the places I want to get to in my self-exploration can happen better with women than men because women are willing to go to a deeper emotional level. Even

though there are a lot of men I like now, they are so outer-directed that they're not really interested in the depth of self-exploration that I want to do.

I certainly can't say that my path won't bring me to a sexual relationship with a man. Even in that case though I can't imagine not continuing to identify as a lesbian. But I think it would be a healing experience on some level if I did have a sexual relationship with a man that was a loving one. But as a partner—I would always want to have a woman partner.

Projective and introjective identifications provide vicarious experiences that may become entries to the unexplored part of the self. Such entries may be predominantly unconscious, occurring largely through unconscious fantasies about the lover: who she is (was) as a heterosexual woman, what she embodies or represents, and what her "possession" of the lover means to her own sense of self, that is, what she has incorporated through the lover. Again, these fantasies may or may not coincide with the lover's actual experiences or sense of self.

The primary lesbian may actively pursue this vicarious experience by exploring with the lover her previous sexual and romantic relationships. Lovers tend to be curious about each other's prior love affairs. When she inquires about her partner's past relationships with men, she is, perhaps quite unconsciously, trying them on herself. She seeks greater understanding of women's sexual and emotional intimacy with men and the sense of self engendered therein. Karen described her interest in Janine's marriage to a man.

Even though I was with men, there's no comparison. I don't know what it's like to be in a relationship with a man of any substance. There's a lot of mystery about that to me. I find myself wondering how that really is because I have such a different perception of relationships with men. It's intriguing. I don't have an interest in it other than curiosity. Especially about Janine's. She had a *very good* relationship with a man. The men I was with were fine, but they weren't magical or anything. So it's unknown, curious, different. It's given me a perception of men I never had, kind of a different slice of the pie [laughs]. A slice I'd never taken a bite of.

Suzanne, a primary lesbian, spoke about Abby's past in a similar way.

How she felt toward men is interesting to me. I have a weird relationship with men because I actually prefer the company of men sometimes, but sexually, well, I felt like it could have been any old doormat underneath, it didn't really matter that it was me, Suzanne. I think what's interesting is that Abby had good sexual relationships with men and I didn't. So it's interesting to hear how she talks about it, that you could feel that way toward men. I don't know if it affected me, but I catalogued it away somewhere. Men have always been someone for me to compete with, in athletics and in school. So it's interesting how Abby relates to men, the whole dynamic is different, like "Oh! What a novel idea!" It's another way to be in the world.

The bisexual lesbian, however, projects onto her lover the unlived, but perhaps unconsciously desired, experience of exclusivity with women. This may include a denied loyalty to the mother or a disowned desire to have remained true to that early love affair (remember Persephone and Demeter). The lover symbolizes an all-female world where men have never intruded. Miriam, extensively bisexual, expressed something of this fantasy when she and her lover Ellen, who had few heterosexual experiences, discussed their differences.

MIRIAM: You seem cleaner, more pure. There's a way that I trust you more. It's like you're more of a virgin in a certain way [laughs].
ELLEN: Virginal!
MIRIAM: My God! This opens up a whole new avenue to our sexuality. You look very nice in white [both laugh]. . . . This is a brand new thought. I felt I always lost with men, that I was the one who gave it up, he was the one who got. There's always been some degree of shame for me about that. So the idea that you haven't been . . . or that you found the whole thing uninteresting . . . it's not like you were grossed out, but that it had a limited impact, like "Who cares?" I haven't put it together before, that that's some of my attraction to you, that there's this sense of purity to you, that you're unsoiled. Hmmm. . . .

The lover is thus an other who carries projected fantasies of existence in that imagined world. The relationship between the couple lets each partner carry these experiences while the other unconsciously identifies with them. Because this pursuit may be largely unconscious for a woman, it may be signified in symbolic ways. For example, Wendy, a bisexual, felt that she gained legitimacy as a lesbian by involvement with a woman who was a primary lesbian. This pursuit may occur through fantasies about the lover's early years. A woman may also actively question her lover about her relationships with other women, about early lesbian experiences, and about the world of

lesbians. I asked Abby how she felt about Suzanne's very early relationship (from ages ten to fourteen) with another girl.

> ABBY: I feel envious. I kept telling her that one of the things in
> the way of my making a commitment was that I never had my
> lesbian adolescence and that I really wanted that. I kept pushing
> her to tell me about her relationship with Elaine.
> Q: What did you want to know?
> ABBY: I wanted to know everything, the details. Was it like sex
> the way we think about sex? Was it kissing? Was it sexual play
> the way I had sexual play with girlfriends, which was more like
> making up games, not kissing. I couldn't understand a ten-year-
> old doing that. I just found it so interesting that she was so
> passionate, that she would ride her bike over to Elaine's and
> climb in her window to sleep overnight there.

Janine, who had long been married, described how she became
aware of her longing for entry into this female world through visual
images that caught her off guard. "I went to a party at Karen's house
before we were involved. I talked to her lover. I went past their
bedroom and saw the bed. I thought that must be so wonderful. . . .
There's a romance to it, a romantic perception about lesbian relationships when you come out late, that you've been yearning for. I saw a
movie with my husband about two women making love, and I cried.
This yearning felt bigger than my whole body. It was the biggest thing,
stored up forever. Walking past the bedroom was like that. That room
was a symbol of it, that yearning. I think she represented that to me."

Alix, who came out in the mid 1980s, said she wished she could
have experienced the period of the early 1970s, when the lesbian
community was tighter, more separatist and enmeshed. For her, such a
community represented a world of women together, gone now, that
she tried to recapture after she came out.

> I missed that period in the seventies of women's music and
> sleeping with everybody's best friend: you know, that whole
> *Peyton Place* syndrome and the little tight community combined
> with a separatist phase. I was living with my boyfriend. It was
> really different for me. When I met Carol, all I could do was play
> Holly Near records, and she would go "Ugh! God, if I ever hear
> another Holly Near record, I'll barf!" and I would feel, "How
> could you?"
> She'd tell me all these stories. She had thousands of associa-
> tions to every song that I was hearing for the first time. It was all
> this stuff that I'd never been in on. I imagine them having this

ten-year period of birth for lesbian-feminism. I see them as very isolated from the heterosexual world, having trouble interacting with men, having contempt for men. Now I see that as changing.

Unconscious Desires, Unconscious Reconciliations

Why do primary and bisexual lesbians seek such exchanges if they find fulfillment in their own experiences? Again, the desire for an Other, different in some personally significant way, is in part a consequence of the frustrations and limitations inherent in human psychology. In the inner world these limitations are simultaneously known and denied. To some extent the unlived potential beckons and entices in the imaginative realm. Sigmund Freud first argued that one's bisexual potential always exists, yet the vicissitudes of both internal and external demands force a direction to be taken.[1] As Kenneth Lewes notes, "any adequate analytic description of an individual would necessarily have to deal with the fate of bisexual strivings and the way they inform both heterosexual and homosexual wishes and behavior."[2] According to psychoanalyst Joyce McDougall,

> In point of fact, every child wants to possess the mysterious sexual organs and fantasized power of *both* parents. And indeed why not? Whether we are male or female, one of the greatest narcissistic wounds of childhood is inflicted by the obligation to come to terms with our ineluctable monosexuality—its scar of course, the problem of what to do with our psychic bisexuality. . . . In the world of dreams we are all magical, bisexual, and immortal! . . . [Universal] homosexual desires in children of both sexes always have a double aim. One is the desire to *possess*, in the most concrete fashion, the parent of the same sex, and the second is the desire to *be* the opposite sex and to possess all the privileges and prerogatives with which the opposite-sex parent is felt to be endowed. . . . Thus the little girl not only wants to possess her mother sexually, create children with her, and be uniquely loved by her in a world from which all men are excluded; she also desires ardently to be a man like her father, to have his genitals as well as the power and other qualities she attributes to him.[3]

In the potential space of the relational world one may partake imaginatively and unconsciously of these foreclosed experiences. To the unconscious, all time is present: past, present, and future are the same. What happened in the past is also happening now, and what happens now may alter or become what happened then. What the future holds is the past, and changing one's idea of the future changes the past. In the psychosexual world of desire, we are always experimenting with what still tugs at us for resolution and consummation. Such desires and possibilities exist in all relationships, of course, not only in lesbian ones.

For a lesbian, there may even be a greater intensity to the search for the unexperienced part of the oedipal relationship. It is not enough that she finds her greatest satisfaction in relationships with other women or that doing so feels right. The deviancy or "perversion" attributed to her desires cannot fail to be internalized. She is told she hates or fears men or that women are inadequate as partners for other women. These often strident judgments may create a greater need to find some psychic counterpart that allows her to experiment with variations on her own experience.

Paula described how this process took place for her. All of her lovers have been lesbians with bisexual pasts; she, however, has never been involved with a man. When she first realized that she loved a woman, she thought the attraction was terrible and resisted. "Then as time went by, I came out. I feel like my coming out process will probably continue until I die. I really feel that way . . . I've always found that the people I like the best are lesbians generally, which has been part of the process by which I've come to love myself—by seeing my reflection in other women and having it come back in a loving way. Really I feel like the process of coming out has been exactly the process of mirroring—being mirrored by women until I got to the point where I could love that part of myself that they mirrored to me."

For Paula, the fact that her lovers related to men but chose women made it clear that it was a positive choice, and she felt valued by them in her womanness. Abby expressed the bisexual counterpart of this experience when she described how her relationship with Suzanne had repaired her sense of self as a woman. She said she is happier now than she had been, feels good about her femaleness, and, paradoxically, is more forgiving of men's shortcomings.

If a woman does have negative responses to men, she can experience the potential of a different kind of relationship through a lover who has enjoyed men. If she herself feels some devaluation of women as partners, she may find a new evaluation of this choice through a woman who has joyously embraced women as lovers. The particular wounds to which lesbian experience is inevitably vulnerable may be redressed in the relationship. Indeed, there may be a "lowered threshold" to projective exchanges in this area.[4]

This type of projective exchange is not based upon ridding oneself of unwanted parts, but quite the opposite. It is a search for wanted but unknown or undeveloped parts of the self. In the unconscious match between partners, each finds an Other who embodies an expression of that desired self. Primary lesbians, for example, may project their unknown potential for heterosexuality onto lovers and see them as intriguing expressions of heterosexual potential, yet still within the familiar territory of lesbianism. Bisexual lesbians project the potential for primary lesbianism onto partners and thereby find it in a form that can be claimed indirectly.

Again, for lesbians, there may even be some greater propensity toward projective exchange. The potential of women, especially those in lesbian relationships, to move toward merging reflects women's more fluid ego boundaries. This fluidity lends itself to the psychological exchange found in complementary projective bonding. Melanie Klein speaks of projective identification as a process in which "the ego takes possession . . . of an external object . . . and makes it an extension of the self."[5] This aspect of projective identification has largely been neglected in explorations of how relationships work. Its role in guiding the self toward objects (an agent of attraction), in sustaining these connections through the mutual identifications engendered (an agent of bonding), and in enriching the self (an agent of transformation) suggests a cumulative power that can explain relationships that endure despite innumerable obstacles.

Complementarity's Shadow

This analysis is weighted toward positive aspects of complementarity. The potential for negative experiences and defensive exchanges is also present. Either or both partners may disown parts of themselves and project them onto the other. When one continues to disown personal conflicts, differences are an ongoing threat. They may persist as unwanted attributes and become a source of external conflict. Partners may carry each other's projections too uncomfortably for transformation to occur.

Differences may also be seen as desired qualities and envied rather than introjected. The positive introjection of attributes may never occur, and identifications may persist in negative ways. What once attracted the partners may become what most disturbs or threatens them. These differences hold the possibility of destroying as well as preserving their bond.

The biggest threat to a relationship, of course, is that the bisexual partner's old interest in men will resurface. To the primary lesbian, this prospect looms as a possibility over which she has no control and threatens a loss that is qualitatively different from the one all relationships face, the dissolution of the relationship. When this interest in men occurs, its effects are long-lasting. Dina said, "I had a very early relationship with a woman who got married immediately after our break-up. This was very painful for me. I think it's probably always left me with some distrust."

The dissolution of a lesbian partnership over a man may feel like a special kind of rejection or negation, requiring special defenses. Most primary lesbians whom I interviewed recalled a period in their lives when they retreated from bisexual women and held ideological positions that condemned lesbians who became involved with men. When I asked Paula, one of the primary lesbians who had never slept with a man, if her lesbianism felt like a choice, she responded:

Now it does. It never used to. As a result I was a political extremist—extremely judgmental of straight women. I couldn't understand why you would sleep with a man and be straight. I ghettoized myself. Basically we were all ghettoizing ourselves. I was certainly of the school that anyone who slept with a man couldn't call herself a lesbian. Bisexuals were traitors. If you were a lesbian who slept with a man, that was it—you were out of the club.
Q: Why has that changed?
PAULA [pausing]: Because I can imagine myself doing it.

Some women spoke of the ways differences in sexual histories create barriers. An alienation exists, similar to that created in heterosexual relationships by differences in gender. As Dina put it, "When I'm with a woman who's had satisfying heterosexual relationships, it makes me feel lonely." Jan, who has always been lesbian but whose partner was married for many years, recounted how her feelings about these differences changed over time:

I used to feel about bisexual women, "Stay away—bad news." I was never very attracted to bisexual women because at that point my gay life was segmented away from my real life. The more normal I made myself in terms of surrounding myself with people who liked me the way I was, the less I had a hang-up about it. You hear a lot of stories about women going to women and then back to be with men. It made me angry, and I wouldn't go near them. Now I don't have those feelings. When I was younger I had a lot more distrust. Then it felt like someone like that wouldn't *understand* me. In fact that's true to a certain extent. They don't understand my situation as well as someone who's grown up that way.

It seems that the threat of complementary differences is heightened when the partnership does not take advantage of them. Marty related how the difference in sexual histories had been a problem with her former partner: "I think she wanted and needed to deny my past heterosexual relationships. I think it was difficult and upsetting for her to think I'd been involved with men. She really didn't like it. As a result I had to not make an issue of it or talk about past relationships. That was uncomfortable. A part of me was not acceptable to her. . . . She was jealous of my interactions with anyone. I think she felt I wasn't safe with anyone. She saw me as pan-sexual, like I could be falling into bed with anyone." The relational exchanges were closed off to them, and the threat grew. In this situation, where the lover is unable to participate in the incorporative dimensions of projective experience, all that remains are the projections. The beloved then embodies not only her own bisexual interests but also the unconsciously projected ones of the lover, and her interest in men is seen as even greater and more threatening. Meanwhile, the lover feels the impossibility of ever bringing her full self into the relationship.

When the potential for exchange is rejected, the lover may herself feel rejected. When her partner finds her experiences unacceptable, she may find them unacceptable herself. Wendy recalled her discomfort in earlier relationships with primary lesbians who had no appreciation of her former relationships with men. "I don't think they particularly wanted to hear about them. And I didn't particularly want to talk about them. . . . I think possibly because they had never been with men or been with men in the same way, I felt kind of embarrassed about it. . . . I remember I used to feel early on, not exactly shame, but embarrassment. It was something I would talk about kind of reluctantly. It was important to seal that off."

One couple felt stress at times because of the partners' different histories. There was clearly an electric connection between the women. They were close and laughed about their differences, but both felt these differences were a major area of conflict. Carol, a primary lesbian, is in her first relationship with a woman with a bisexual past, and it is Carol's most enduring relationship. It is Alix's first relationship with a woman; she was married for ten years and has two children.

CAROL: I never have struggled with anyone this way before, but I never was with anyone who wanted so much intimacy. The kids change it too. We aren't just two independent adults. We were thrown into this nurturing family unit. I couldn't get involved with them any quicker because I had to protect myself. I could really get hurt. It wouldn't have been good for them either if I'd jumped in too quickly. I wasn't going to be a parent right away. And now I'm clearly a parent. I don't know. . . . I can't separate the person from the history. If that's what made her want the intimacy with me. . . .

ALIX: The first three months we were together I wouldn't let you get out of bed. You kept saying you wanted to thank those men. She was writing thank you cards.

CAROL: I couldn't believe it! I was in heaven.

ALIX: See, there's something good about it. You can still thank those men for that. It hasn't worn off.

CAROL: It's made me aware of my edges and boundaries. There was a lot of homophobia, some real hard times. But when I was defending myself I needed to do that. It makes me more aware of myself, the differences.

Q: So maybe it's not coincidental to your being together?

ALIX: She's certainly not who I was looking for.

CAROL: She was looking for someone cosmopolitan. . . . And I was never attracted to straight-looking and acting women. And look at you!

ALIX: I relate to Carol's loneliness because I feel lonely too that she doesn't share my heterosexual past.

CAROL: There's a gulf between us that's always there. I never felt that with my other lovers. Maybe now that I've finally found someone who really wants intimacy, I have to fight her off. Maybe I would have created more of a gulf with these women of similar backgrounds if there really was a chance for intimacy. . . . But there is a way that I feel you don't know me . . . and that I don't know you.

ALIX: That makes me sad.

CAROL: Yeah.

ALIX: It has to be there somewhere.

Clearly such profound differences as sexual history and orientation do not simply hold a potential bond. Like all differences that really matter, they are both intriguing and unappealing. They create alienation as well as complementarity, and sometimes both, within the same relationship. The question is, How the psyche can put such differences to use? If there is enough receptivity to the untapped part of the self for the psyche to risk the exploration, then opportunity prevails for the enrichment brought about only through love.

Conclusion

For some of the women in this study, the differences in sexuality—feelings, fantasies, and behavior—between them and their lovers were striking, meaningful, and challenging. These differences required the women to span what had been untraveled psychosexual territory. They had not consciously chosen partners who were different, but neither could they dismiss their choices as coincidental. Such choices represent a need, usually unconscious, to explore unlived parts of one's own potential through relationships with others who have taken alternate routes.

Not all of the couples or individuals I interviewed felt that their differences in this territory were meaningful. The complementarity of this particular difference is deeply rooted in unconscious experience, and therefore I had expected that it would be hard to identify and articulate. As the interviews progressed, I realized that another factor was also at work. This psychosexual dimension depends in one way or another upon whether a woman feels a sense of alienation from men (heterosexual men in particular) and whether that is an issue for her, consciously or unconsciously. If a primary lesbian has had no positive sexual or social experiences with men, the presence of men in her lover's life or history probably carries a more charged meaning for her than would be the case otherwise. If she has resolved her relationships with men in a way that is satisfactory to her, such a presence may matter less.

On the other hand, some bisexual lesbians had already had considerable experience with other women before their present relationships. Desire for access to a world of women, fantasies about women who have not been so meaningfully involved with men, and whatever else this difference signifies may hold less psychological interest for these women. Even within a current relationship, initial interest may have diminished so that this difference lingers as a curious, but not compelling, phenomenon.

The psychosexual attraction of differences between lesbians affords the opportunity to experience a road not previously taken. For some women, this road looks forbidding; their relationship to their unexplored sexual potential is alienated, and their attraction to it may be simultaneously powerful and threatening. For others, it is simply intriguing, an opportunity for a relational adventure. The dialectical possibilities for complementary exchanges invite each woman, perhaps unconsciously, perhaps with some awareness, to rework her relationship to her own sense of sexual self. Vicariously she comes to know more intimately a broader range of the human sexual potential. These exchanges fulfill the promise of relationship and offer each partner some new frontier for self-experience.

Over the years, differences get smoothed out. A couple that stays together no longer feels or seems so different from each other as they did at the beginning of their relationship. Their views of themselves and each other alter with time. The primary lesbian may put a different emphasis on her history; she may give more weight to early sexual experiences with men and begin to see herself as more bisexual than she once did. The bisexual lesbian may do the reverse. She may give less credit to her relationships with men and reevaluate early relationships with girlfriends. She then identifies a more primarily lesbian part of her sexuality.

People constantly rewrite their personal histories as they rediscover lost parts or wear out the meanings of others. The differences that distinguish partners may crumble over time. New dimensions for exchange are then sought, and new interpretations of the relationship emerge.

Deviant Selves and
Different Selves

7 | The lesbian whose identity develops in adolescence generally must cope with a profound sense of social difference. How she handles this dilemma will to some extent determine her later experiences. Homosexual studies recognize that this confrontation can be traumatizing. Vivian Cass asserts that ability to tolerate being different is the crucial determinant of whether a young lesbian will develop a healthy identity or whether she will resort to denial.[1] Homosexual studies provide no clues, however, to what makes such tolerance possible for one person and not for another. Psychoanalytic theory, even while it argues that lesbianism is pathological, also posits that an ability to face differences is a major developmental achievement, one that draws upon early successes in the interpersonal matrix of parent-child relationships. The course of sexual identity development clearly calls for some integration of social theories with psychodynamic ones.

The developmental paths for primary and bisexual lesbians shape these women's lives in rather opposite ways. When they join paths later in an intimate relationship, they find their complement in each other. An adolescent lesbian manages the experience of deviancy one way or another, but the experience can leave scars. Alliance with a partner who is closer to the mainstream eases her sense of alienation. Meanwhile, her ability to tolerate such a difference is attractive to later-developing lesbians who question their own capacity for being different. One must bridge internal and external dimensions of sexual development to understand the interplay between them in lesbian relationships.

Dealing with Deviance

The second dimension of complementarity in lesbian relationships is already suggested by the first one, psychosexual differences. The sense of self as deviant is likely to be experienced somewhat differently by women who have such diverse histories of sexual experience. While the fundamentals of social identity are developed in adolescence, a primary lesbian has two other interrelated tasks. She must find within herself the strength to tolerate deviancy when social conformity is most highly valued. She must also, usually in isolation, evaluate the social construction of what is acceptable sexual behavior.

Will she deny her felt sexual inclinations? Will she accept herself as lesbian but perverse? Will she come to perceive herself as disturbed on even broader dimensions, feeling that something is wrong with her very being? Or will she manage rather independently to affirm her identity and to assert that the culture's evaluation is somehow wrong? What defenses will be required to accomplish this enormous task, and how much of her psychic resources will then be tied up in self-protection?

Dina, an early lesbian, talked about how she drew upon other experiences of being different to help handle such a significant difference. "I was different in other ways as a kid. I was the only out and out tomboy. I was very athletic and competent physically. My parents were radicals in a working-class Catholic neighborhood. They seemed more courageous and more intelligent than the others. They were atheists. The other mothers stayed home more. So my family was different and that was positively imbued. When I came out to my parents I used the family's differences to support my right to be gay."

On the other hand, Fran, a woman who came out in her forties after sixteen years of marriage and three children, discussed how her experience with feeling different when she was young did not help her later.

> I was told by my mother that I was special and not like the other children, smarter, things like that. I held myself to be different from my peers. This was supposed to be good, but really I just felt shy and socially awkward. I felt like an oddball. I read a lot and had more adult interests. I didn't fit in anywhere. I imagine that lesbians who came out when they were younger had a rougher time though, feeling outside the social pale. In adulthood I entered the mainstream. I was no longer the oddball and that helped me form a kind of core identity. I recouped my early losses. This made a big difference to me.

When Fran came out as a lesbian, finding a place in the mainstream still prevailed as a concern. Her choice of lovers effected a compromise about her dilemma. She first had affairs with women who also identified with heterosexual experience, yet who had come out ten to fifteen years before she did. This balance was important because it bridged being different and fitting in.

Alix also discussed how she bridges the two worlds within herself, and how she and her lover Carol learn from each other.

> My position of being a formerly heterosexual lesbian is a great joy to me. No regrets about having been straight. It allows me to interact with the world in a way that's very important to me. We fight about that. She works for this small liberal company, and they're like a family. I demand to be a part of that family, just like any other partner. They include everybody anyway, but what's important is that I demand it inside me. She expects straight people to be homophobic. She's in a defensive stance, and I'm just the opposite. If anything, maybe I need to get a little smarter, be a little less naive and look at the underside of what liberal people are saying. And she needs to be a little more demanding or assertive.

The more primary lesbian may have first experienced her own sexuality as normal; her love for a woman felt natural. Later experiences may have altered this sense. If she is involved in a relationship with a lover who has not been so deviant, who seems to fit mainstream requirements for sexuality better than she and yet also chooses women, she may project and re-find the original sense that loving a woman is natural. The lover may have emerged from adolescence relatively unscathed (in this sense) as she participated in the usual heterosexual encounters and did not think her sexuality to be abnormal. She becomes an embodiment of normality that includes loving other women.

On the other side of the equation, the previously heterosexual woman finds a partner who has tolerated being different and can lead her into a new capacity for the same in herself. The new lover's ability to tolerate such a sense of deviancy may be a source of attraction when the bisexual woman questions whether she would (or could) have done what the lover did. If she knows (consciously or unconsciously) that she lacks further development in this aspect of her personality, the relationship offers both impetus and support for doing so.

During the course of the interviews, the subject of deviancy touched more anxiety, anger, and painful memories than any other subject. This was especially true for several primary lesbians, who recalled years of self-doubt, inner chaos, and social ostracism that they had not thought about for a long time. Carol, an early lesbian, described the shock to her self-image and then to her social image. "I couldn't figure out how I could be gay. I'd never done anything wrong or bad in my life and here I was. I had to deal with all these feelings that it was wrong or bad and trying to figure out why. I thought if I could explain it to people, then they wouldn't hate me. I spent my whole senior year trying to figure it out." Carol expressed her thoughts about bisexual lesbians or those who come out later in life.

> Those who come out late—they're "normal." They're privileged in the sense that they had it easy. They know what it's like to be fully accepted and to be fully normal and to feel it. If they really were in love with someone of the opposite sex, they have the privilege of not always feeling different. I feel like they just don't know what it's like. It's like growing up rich and not knowing what it's like being poor.
>
> You don't realize what it feels like to be forced to bend a way you're not bending naturally. You can overcome that as an adult, but you can't change that you went through it. I think people who grew up straight and then became gay, I don't think they understand that.

Sometimes the bisexual lesbians expressed feelings of guilt, a kind of survivor's guilt, that they had managed to escape the experiences their lovers had endured. Often these women were keenly aware that at certain junctures in their lives they had avoided confronting their interest in other women. Maggie described her own coping and failure to deal with being different when she was younger.

> It's not like it [lesbianism] wasn't a known thing. I was in the feminist movement in Berkeley in the 1970s. Everyone was coming out. So it's not like it wasn't an option. . . . I'd always known I was bisexual. It was more a matter of what did I want? I didn't want to add external forms of oppression to what was already inside. What did I want? Just to be accepted in the world. The main thing I was looking for was someone whose car would be in the driveway when I got home. I got married and moved to the suburbs and had kids. He was a loving man. He had a normal loving family who embraced me. So I was buying into a whole package. I really wanted to have kids. . . . I like to talk about this now because it makes me realize the ways my current relationship breaks all the rules.

What Other People Think

The issue of dealing with difference recalls feminist psychoanalytic revisions of female development that discuss how difficult it may be for women to handle difference.[2] Differences do not establish gender identity for women as they do for men. They present a threat to the sense of oneness in relationship that is more characteristic of women's psychological experience. Separateness and differentation remain problematic in female development, just as their opposite, intimacy, may be a greater source of trouble in male development.

Women may fear differences and, almost as a corollary, fear being different themselves. The pressure to conform, to please, to meet others' expectations arises from this fear and can determine the shape of a woman's life. Socialization into culturally based modes of femininity compound the pressure, especially in adolescence. As Emily Hancock observes, "Conformity marks the era of the older girl. . . . Impressed with the importance of others' opinions, she molds herself to be what she thinks they want her to be."[3]

Yet difference, or otherness, is inescapable. Finding a comfortable way of incorporating differentness (one's own or others') is a continuing theme in women's adult development. Again, we encounter a paradox in the course of lesbian development. Early development both fosters and requires a sense of difference. Ability to traverse this course depends upon the girl's capacity for tolerating difference. In some respects the early lesbian has a developmental advantage; she is challenged to incorporate differentness within her sense of self. Even if the process is by its nature defensive, as it is for men, she emerges with greater familiarity and ease with differentness. A woman whose sexual identity comes later, after adolescence, encounters the primary lesbian with respect. She is drawn to her as an embodiment of what is missing within herself. She senses the possibility of continuing the task and seeks a connection with the primary lesbian and thus immerses herself in the experience of differentness.

For two of the couples this issue defined their relationship more clearly than any other. The bisexual lesbians in both relationships talked about the importance of their lovers' abilities to resist the pull of conformity. Both felt a strong need to fit into mainstream culture, and both thought that caring about the opinion of others had shaped them far more than they liked. For each, the lover's strength in defining herself so early held a powerful attraction. When I asked Miriam what was important about this difference between her and Ellen, she said, "It has to do with not caring as much, in the way that *I'm* familiar with, about what other people think of you. For me, what other people think is of primary significance. That's the way I think. I wish I didn't. There's something very, very attractive to me about someone who's not set up that way. I see that as a strength, a kind of confidence and strength. It would be such a relief not to think as much about things that way. So I guess you connect with people that make up for something that's lacking in you. I appreciate her strength." Abby also described her attraction to Suzanne along the same lines. "What she brought to this relationship was an incredible ego, an incredible sense of self that I was lacking. It really helped me. She has a strong ego and doesn't need a lot of external approval. She does what she thinks is right for herself and doesn't need anybody to like it. That's not so for me."

In both relationships the partners thought their lovers overstated their invulnerability to social approval, again suggesting that to some degree lovers make of each other what they need for their own sense of complementarity. For example, Abby's lover, Suzanne, described how she became a cheerleader in her adolescence because her mother had become more and more distressed with her. She concealed her lesbian affairs from her peers at school. She recognized that what others thought of her did matter; it simply did not determine her fundamental choices.

ABBY: If somebody wants to tell her what they think of her, then she feels "screw 'em."
SUZANNE: That's not true.
ABBY: Well, pretty much. And that's something I admire in you.
SUZANNE: Of course I want people to like me, and I want them to approve of me.
ABBY: But you won't change your behavior to suit them.
SUZANNE: If it feels honest, then it's acceptable to me. I don't need to know what other people think. For Abby, she needs to know what other people think and feel about it. She gathers information. I'm not saying that's bad or good. In fact I've learned a lot from her about how to distill my feelings through talking with other people, friends. I think both of us have grown from the combination of the two. I've helped Abby become more independent, trust her feelings and her intuition more. Certainly she makes decisions faster than she used to. And I'm not so much of an island. I'm connecting more with people and finding out about how they feel, and in so doing I've shared how I feel and that's the really growthful part for me.

For Ellen and Miriam, the questions about dealing with difference led to a discussion that brought small revelations to each.

ELLEN: The women I've been attracted to would pass in a straight world. . . . I'm not sure what's going on there.

Q: It seems like you're saying the counterpart of what Miriam said. She said you're not interested in passing, yet you're saying you're attracted to women who can.

ELLEN: That's true. I hadn't thought of them as being connected.

MIRIAM: Part of what you love about bringing me to your family is that I make you more acceptable because they can relate to me. What you find attractive is someone who is more . . . ?

ELLEN: In the fold. . . . It's an interesting idea. Basically I gave up caring about fitting in. I understood at some point that that was not going to work for me, and that what was more important for me was to find meaningful relationships rather than to be acceptable.

MIRIAM: But the women you chose fit in much better than you do.

ELLEN: Right. Maybe it is my attempt to get back in somehow, to get some sense of belonging.

MIRIAM [to me]: It's so weird. She doesn't think that way. It wouldn't occur to her.

ELLEN: It would have to be a subconscious thing . . .

MIRIAM: Because the motivation of "what people think" is irrelevant.

ELLEN: It's not exactly irrelevant. I've just chosen not to regulate my life around it. It isn't as important as other things. But it's in everybody, the need to belong.

MIRIAM [laughs]: You mean you have it too?

ELLEN [also laughing]: Somewhere. . . .

For both Ellen and Suzanne, coming out in their early years was not as traumatic as it had been for some of the other primary lesbians to whom I spoke. Both grew up in liberal West Coast communities that were more tolerant of a variety of sexual behaviors. Perhaps in such circumstances the stress of being different falls into an optimal range that challenges without overwhelming the individual. Women who can draw upon previous developmental achievements may, under these conditions, grow into a capacity for being different that leaves them less dependent upon others' approval, even as adolescents. Yet they still have a sense of missing out on important experiences. Miriam and Ellen summarized the mutuality of their influence upon each other.

MIRIAM: I've seen you change in becoming more a part of the world, caring more, being more engaged, belonging more.

ELLEN: Yes. And I think you have facilitated that, you've eased it

a little bit, partly because *you* do it so well. Just being with you, I get into it. You make me a little more acceptable in certain ways.
MIRIAM: There's a real dialectic here. The more she becomes more acceptable, the more I'm comfortable not fitting in. I've been much more comfortable being out, being affectionate. It's funny.

An exchange with Alix and Carol expresses the same issues.

ALIX: I think people are together in order to work out what they have to work out as much as for any other reason. That's the only way to get any happier, is to clear away some debris . . . I feel we challenge each other because of our differences. Where I position myself in the straight world—that's certainly different than who she's been with before. And she's less ghettoized than she used to be. I can only assume for her to be with someone for five years who's never been ghettoized—well, there has to be a reason for it. And for me with her too, to deal with that oppression. At certain times I've thought, "Wouldn't it be easier to be with one of my bisexual friends, and we could have all these common-alities and pass together if we needed to, and not have the damage of oppression that afflicts some life-long lesbians." But I needed to clean some stuff up for myself about homophobia and feeling different. So I think even though the same differences that cause us so much struggle and strife from day to day and cause us each to feel lonely and misunderstood sometimes also have been a big part of the growth for me.
Q [to Carol]: What do you think of that?
CAROL: I think it's probably true. I never had this craving to pass or look more straight because of my whole thing about being drawn to androgyny. I feel pretty much comfortable with who I am. Given that I never would have sought to look straight or even to have a straight-looking lover, I've noticed the privilege of walking down the street arm in arm with someone who looks straight. Alix was the first who claimed that, the privilege of being out and open and that gave me the option. Her, not having known hiding ever, and me, having known only hiding. Before, I was out, but only because I had ghettoized myself. I never was out publicly, on the streets. I don't think I ever held hands with a lover in public before, and now I do it all the time without even thinking. That's a major benefit. I don't know whether I would have worked that out for myself. It's a lot easier doing it with someone who looks straight.

Again, this complementarity has a shadowy side. Alix also described how she has been unable to claim the authenticity that Carol feels about her identity.

> I feel alienated, like I'm not a "real lesbian." I've got a heavy dose internally of being phony or fake. I got this in my family, which was Jewish but passed. I suffer from the impostor syndrome wherever I go. I'm not like other lesbians, for example, because I don't have ex-lovers. That's a really big thing. They're all male. I feel resentful about that. You know there's this stuff about lesbians having extended families, and when we're old we'll all be sitting on the porch rocking with our ex-lovers. And there's only one way for me to get ex-lovers, and that's not appealing to me. I feel very different. This weekend we were with some friends who've been lesbian for at least fifteen years, and one of them said to me, "My God, you don't have ex-lovers!" It was like I was missing my right arm.

Miriam, who idealized Ellen's nonchalance about fitting in, also admitted that she sometimes hates it. "It feels like it's going to diminish me in some way, for her not to care. I'm working on this. But it's like people are going to find me less acceptable if she's less acceptable."

The Press Toward Merger

The question of difference also raises the complex question of the relationship between merger and complementarity. Because many writers have regarded merger or fusion as a major issue in clinical work with lesbian couples, the theme has tended to dominate the picture of lesbian psychology.[4] Merger goes beyond mere closeness or attachment. It is a sense of *being* the other person rather than being like, connected to, or near the other. With merger, the metaphorical boundary between self and other is changed or dissolved, and a sense of union overtakes the sense of separateness.

At its most intense and pleasurable, falling in love is the quintessential experience of merger. Love-making is, in part, a pursuit of this psychic union. The loving gaze, the desire to touch, and the sense of silent communion that lovers share create and recreate a feeling of oneness. These heightened experiences of merger bring a sense of transformation, as one feels utterly changed, renewed, or expanded. According to Ethel Person, "the fluidity of the ego enables the kind of interpenetration of selves that constitutes merger. . . . [T]he exaltation of love is most of all attributable to the new expanded sense of self that results when two separate beings come together as one. In large measure, exaltation is made possible by the lovers' periodic achievement of 'merger,' with its sense of release from the burdens of the self, the immersion in something larger than self."[5]

However, merger is not entirely defined by this exalted state. A more mundane (and less conscious) merger exists in a daily way for many couples. This is the merger of couples who have difficulty feeling or being separate from each other, who have to think in terms of each other with every move, who in fact feel guilty or anxious about interests, thoughts, and feelings that are *not* shared. Their individual selves have been given over to fusion, and they may feel it is a necessity of the relationship not to retrieve them.

While many, if not all, intimate relationships, including friendships, probably involve experiences of merger, a prolonged or enduring fusion is ultimately destructive both to the individual sense of self and to the relationship. The couple founders in a mesh of too much connectedness. One or both partners eventually feels the loss of self and tries to emerge from the overly close union, but rarely is this possible without disruption of the relationship.

Women who seek to reestablish their sense of self make desperate efforts to create a boundary by highlighting their differences instead of their similarities, by provoking fights, by sexually or emotionally withdrawing, by having an affair, or by leaving the relationship altogether. A balance of intimate connection with autonomy cannot be found within the individuals or within the relationship. This is the picture therapists often describe from clinical practice.[6]

Current thinking about women's developmental issues emphasizes the importance of relatedness for women.[7] Jean Baker Miller, Janet Surrey, and other women from the Stone Center at Wellesley College, oppose the perspective held by Nancy Chodorow and other object-relations theorists to the extent that it retains an emphasis on achieving separateness as an essential developmental task. In their view, a woman's self is always a self-in-relation. They do not concur with Chodorow's view that women's more fluid relational ego boundaries constitute a liability as well as an asset. They find that women's embeddedness in interrelatedness is not problematic; it signifies a difference between women's and men's development.[8] Their viewpoint idealizes women's development. At the same time, the Stone Center group makes the point that when women are viewed through male developmental theories, one sees pathology rather than difference.

Although the disagreements between the two feminist psychodynamic perspectives are important, there is agreement that women develop most fully within the matrix of their relatedness to others, not apart from it. Women's sense of individuality must be found within this matrix, not outside of it as may be the case for men. The emphasis on the centrality of attachment, relatedness, and interdependence as issues in women's development explains why these issues reverberate in lesbian relationships. This relational-orientation in women's psychology is expressed, for example, in the tendency of lesbians to maintain ties to former lovers, a phenomenon not so common in heterosexual relationships.[9] Both the value of attachment and the discomfort with separation are manifested.

Heterosexual women and lesbians experience a less-separate sense of self than men of either sexual orientation. The phenomenon of merger in lesbian relationships may indicate a fundamental difference between men and women. That is, it represents different lines in gender development, not in the development of object choice or homosexuality versus heterosexuality. If a greater vulnerability to merger is a consequence of women's early development, then it easily follows that merger would often be manifested in lesbian relationships.[10] The fact that lesbian couples share the same gender invites an illusion of a more total sameness between the partners. Because both are women, the desire for oneness and the fear of its regressive pull create dynamic tension. Differences, real or projectively created, may be threatening, but they are also pursued. Such a complex experience is not easily untangled.

The formulation has other implications as well. It suggests that a relationship between two women that is characterized by merger is not inherently a troubled one. The greater fluidity of women's ego boundaries allows greater intimacy. More psychological work is also required to establish or maintain a sense of self that is not entirely at the whims of relationship.

The value of merger in a relationship between two women has been formulated in other ways as well. Valory Mitchell begins with "the premise that all important relationships derive their importance from permeability of the boundaries of the self so that the loved object is included within . . . performing important *intra*personal functions." Because lesbian relationships may value and seek more closeness than other relationships, Mitchell argues, theories of lesbian dynamics must allow for this difference. "Researchers and clinicians interested in lesbian relationships need a conceptual language and psychological theory that are compatible with the strong relational values and expectations of lesbian clients and research subjects. . . . an over-emphasis on the need for autonomy and separateness can carry an implicit devaluing of lesbian relationships altogether. . . . The ability to open the boundaries of the self, in this theory, is far from pathological. Rather, it is seen as the basis for profound relationship and the necessary condition for psychological growth."[11]

Another positively imbued view of merger comes from the work of the Stone Center. Julie Mencher argues that merger is normative for lesbians, not problematic. It represents the kind of intimacy pattern desired by women in general and is one of the benefits of lesbian relationships. Unfortunately, Mencher does not distinguish between intimacy and merger; her examples of merger do not necessarily involve fusion of self and other, but are characterized by "mutual engagement, mutual empathy, and mutual empowerment."[12] This idealized description does not correspond to the relational dynamics that others have described, which generate anxiety rather than satisfaction. Like Mitchell, however, Mencher makes the important point that "embeddedness" in relationship is desirable to many women and that comparing lesbian relationships to heterosexual ones, which embody different desires and needs, is likely to yield a distorted perception of lesbians.

Some empirical support for the notion that merging between women is not pathological and may enhance development is found in Joan Berzoff's study of heterosexual women friends. Women who reported the most intense experiences of merger or threatened loss of identity in the relationship with their best friend, Berzoff found, also obtained the highest scores on measurements of ego development, indicating highly developed autonomous functioning. Unlike Mencher, however, Berzoff notes the temporary nature of this progressive merger. "Empathy and access to the deepest inner experiences of others requires a high level of self differentiation. Traditional theories which have held that finding oneself means moving away from others do not fully account for adult women's experiences of empathy and connectedness. . . . Such temporary losses of self need to be understood not as regressive or pathological losses, but as potential articulations of the self in the context of an intimate other."[13]

These different views of its function and relative value suggest that the concept of merger needs further delineation. Perhaps merger can be thought of as having at least two dimensions: intensity and fluidity. An intense, rigidly maintained fusion reflects extremes of both dimensions and indicates a pathological incapacity for separateness, while a more fluid but nevertheless deep merger may be inherent in any passionate intimacy. A fixed but less intense merger signifies a relational stalemate that may eventually tolerate some degrees of autonomy. Weak and highly fluid experiences of merger probably occur with great frequency in encounters with friends, lovers, and family members. Between lie the many variations, and their relative benefits and relative psychological risks.

Identity Differences and Merger

Merger relies upon a sense of complementarity. One joins oneself to another, crossing the boundary between self and other through projective and introjective processes, a union offering a greater sense of wholeness or completion. When merger is defensive or protracted, it is experienced as a loss of self rather than an enlargement of self. Projections take over and cannot be contained and processed; the lover feels changed in unwanted ways by the relationship. It is as if she becomes an Other to herself, experiencing a loss of self beyond the transient possibility of transcendance. As Ethel Person observes, "One may seek merger, but one seeks it with an Other. . . . The concrete fulfillment of fantasies of merger carries with it the threat of the symbolic annihilation of the self *and* of the Other. Love, by its nature committed to the preservation of the beloved as well as the self, cannot press through to its goal."[14]

When complementary union is not defensive in origin but derives from a developmental thrust—in which the self is enlarged rather than defenses reinforced—differences between partners are tolerated and ultimately desired. They may, in fact, balance the pull toward merger. A delicate tension between the interplay of sameness and difference occurs in lesbian relationships. Both aspects are attractive and yet hold distinct hazards. The sameness in early development and gender-related experiences offers many opportunities for intimacy and mutual identification—fertile ground for projective exchange.

At the same time, differences foster a need for creative tension. The variations of lesbian orientation provide this tension in ways that hold significant potential for continuing development. Here the discussion is more positively weighted because these possibilities have been neglected in earlier studies. Several women interviewed spontaneously surmised that the differences in sexual orientation between themselves and their partners seemed at times to serve this positive function. Marty, for example, did not think that she and her lover had very different sexual histories, but nevertheless thought that each viewed the sexual attractiveness of men differently. Even though Marty prefers relationships with women, she is actually more attracted in a purely sexual way to men, while this is not true of her partner. She said of the difference, "I think I like us to be different. I don't want us to be the same person, and it's nice in that sense. One thing that I think is difficult in women's relationships is the capacity to become too enmeshed, too much the same. And it is a thing that defines us as somewhat different. It is probably nice for that. I don't think it's been a problem."

Carol and Alix described their problems with differences. Alix recognized her tendency to invite merger and to erect the barricades against it at the same time.

> ALIX: I tend to get angry at someone and find fault with them when I'm trying not to feel as close to them as I already do. When we first got together I picked at a lot of things about Carol. I used to take the tack that I could mold the person I was with. . . . Carol was very resistent from the beginning and still is. That's one of the things I love and hate about her. There was a lot of that—me just assuming that if I wanted her to grow her hair long like mine, she'd have long hair.
> CAROL: Right. Any day now.
> ALIX: I just have some dim awareness that I'm probably not going to be able to tell you what to do. [to me] She's breaking me in.

They discussed their tendency to blur the boundaries between them as an example of merger and thought the great difference in their sexual history, something they can neither change nor deny, has the advantage of reminding them often of their distinctness. Carol said, "It's made me aware of my edges and boundaries. It makes me more aware of myself, the difference between us." Wendy spoke in a similar way about her relationship with a woman who is a primary lesbian: "I think it gives us a means not to be so glommed up. It's such a different experience. It feels like there's a separation that comes with it. I don't know quite what I mean but the experience feels so very different."

Conclusion

Relationship is a means of expanding the self through affiliation with an other who embodies a difference of particular significance to the self. The desire for a particular kind of other is likely to be unconscious but not necessarily inaccessible to awareness. Through intimate exchanges, differences that feel alien to the self become somewhat demystified. Some of the women I interviewed found the subject of social deviancy especially salient to their relationships. Most had some painful associations to the topic and felt that it intertwined with other issues in their relationships. The capacity or incapacity to tolerate deviation from others' expectations had shaped their lives, in one way or another, and remained an issue with significant domain in their self-image. The relationship was valued as the place where they could encounter their opposite and thus further encounter themselves.

Knowledge of the partners' contrary histories was often recognized for its full complexity. The inevitable differentiation created between the women was a blessing on some days and a curse on others. Many named the problem of merger as a risk endemic to couples and welcomed their differences as a means to keep a relational stalemate at bay. This awareness ameliorated the painfulness of interpersonal conflicts.

The particular dimensions considered so far, unconscious psychosexual configurations and the acceptance of difference, represent important developmental thrusts that persist unconsciously in everyone throughout adulthood. For some of these women, the mediation of difference was the most important, most deeply felt, aspect of their complementarity. They knew its significance right away and seized upon it as a defining principle in their interpersonal dynamics. It was recognized as an especially fertile area of attraction, exchange, bonding, and, ultimately, growth.

What Gender Signifies

8 The question of gender-related complementarity in lesbian couples remains. If lesbians do not typically engage in role-playing, if no one is the butch and no one the femme, is there no gender interplay between women in relationships with each other? Are lesbians' gender attitudes and identities no different than other women's? Do most lesbians feel traditionally feminine and comfortable with female roles? It seems unlikely. (Do most heterosexual women?) Even if they do eschew roles, do more lesbians identify as masculine than other women? Perhaps. This chapter returns to the question of gender identity and the variations on conventional gender alignments that lesbians may or may not embody.

Confusion over the difference between "sexual identity" (identity as homosexual, bisexual, or heterosexual) and "gender identity" (identity as masculine or feminine) began with sexologists' treatment of the terms *sexual orientation*, *sex roles*, and *gender identity* as roughly synonymous and so congruent developmentally that there was little need to distinguish among them. John Money developed the distinctions between sex and gender into the terms *gender identity* (an internal experience) and *gender role* (a more public, behavioral expression of identity). Robert Stoller attempted another level of distinction by introducing the concept of core gender identity, one's clarity of knowledge that one is a girl or a boy, generally understood to be consolidated around eighteen months of age and relatively immutable after that.[1] Transsexuals, for example, have a core gender identity at odds with their anatomical sex.

My concern is the individual sense of masculinity or femininity, which may be experienced somewhat independently of both core gender identity or sex-role behavior. For example, a woman may have a rather masculine sense of herself even though she definitely identifies herself as female (rather than feminine) and does not wish to be a man. Her behavior may in many ways conform to prescribed female behavior. Nevertheless, she identifies herself as more masculine, or at least as not very feminine. Some writers—including myself—use "gender identity" or "gender role identity" in this way, to refer to the individual's own sense of self as masculine or feminine.

Although all of these terms are now more widely recognized as distinct but related concepts, many psychoanalysts have continued to treat them as essentially congruent. For example, Phyllis Tyson traces distinct development lines for core gender identity, gender role, and object choice, but thinks it appropriate to lump them together under the concept of "global" gender identity: "These separate strands join together and intermingle to make up what we view globally as 'gender identity.'"[2] For her, a homosexual male always expresses femininity, and a lesbian inevitably expresses masculinity, simply by virtue of their object choices. This approach has not progressed very far from the Victorian era of Havelock Ellis.

Contemporary analytic theorists of lesbian development continue to associate gender identity with sexual orientation.[3] In their terms there is no true female-to-female or male-to-male homosexuality. There is only a male-identified woman choosing a woman, or a female-identified man choosing a man. True homosexuality does not really exist, only disguised heterosexuality.[4]

Gender identity is defined here as "a gendered sense of self," or "an internal self-evaluation of maleness or femaleness" distinct from Stoller's idea of core gender identity which is a "recognition of belonging to a biological category."[5] Psychoanalytic and other psychological theories argue that gender identity is based on identification with a given parent, who may or may not be the same sex as oneself.[6] Social constructionists understand gender to be developed in social interactions throughout one's life based on prevailing cultural categories.[7] Thus the question of gender identification that I discuss here is a largely conscious one, determined by shifting identifications with parents and other significant early figures and by social interactions and experience. The conceptual relationship between sexual orientation, sexual identity, gender identity, and sex roles remains ill-defined. The traditional assumption—that as any one of these variables is known, the others then follow—rested upon once-secure cultural assumptions that have become highly insecure, especially with respect to masculinity, femininity, and sex roles.

Because their cultural determinants are in flux, the relationship of these concepts is yet to be reconceived fully. Still, they cannot be treated as entirely separate lines of development. For example, many lesbians, primary and bisexual, describe themselves as being tomboys when they were young, or as being not properly feminine in some way. (Again, this inevitably raises the question of whether many heterosexual women also have felt not typically feminine.) Awareness of gender improprieties often precedes awareness of sexual interests. It may be that this experience shapes or reinforces sexual choices in some way without exactly determining it. At the same time, surely the reverse is true. Awareness of lesbian interests affects one's gendered self-image in some way, although not one that is easily predictable.

Postmodern feminist and Lacanian psychoanalytic thinkers challenge such categorizing, arguing that the category of gender itself is entirely a social construction, the terms of which are decreed by patriarchal law. As Jane Flax observes:

> In Western culture as in most others, gender is a differentiated and asymmetric division and attribution of human traits and capacities. Through gender relations two types of persons are created: males and females, each posited as an exclusionary category. One can be only one gender, rarely the other or both. The actual content of being male or female and the rigidity of the categories themselves are highly variable across cultures and time. There are also many important differences between women (and between men). Nevertheless gender relations so far as we have been able to understand them have been (more or less) relationships of domination.[8]

Judith Butler notes that feminist object-relations theorists attempt to integrate the split between male and female spheres, representing autonomy and nurturance respectively, whereas other feminist psychoanalytic writers (presumably like those theorists associated with the Stone Center) establish the feminine as an alternative, as a subject who defines herself relationally and is different from the masculine because she does not fear dependency. Either approach conceives of "a normative model of a unified self," androgynous in the one case, specifically feminine ("organized by a founding maternal identification") in the other, but a coherent, unified, gendered self either way.[9]

Instead, Butler attempts a radical deconstruction of gender. She negates the idea of a core or coherent gender identity, replacing it with a fluidity of identities. "Gendered identities emerge and sexual desires shift and vary so that different 'identifications' come into play depending upon the availability of legitimating cultural norms and opportunities. . . . Within the terms of psychoanalytic theory, then, it is quite possible to understand gendered subjectivity as a history of identifications, parts of which can be brought into play in given contexts and which, precisely because they encode the contingencies of personal history, do not always point back to an internal coherence of any kind." This possibility, she points out, is expressed through such gender parodies as drag performance (or, I would add, butch-femme identities). "In imitating gender, drag implicitly reveals the imitative structure of gender itself. . . . The notion of gender parody here does not assume that there is an original which such parodic identities imitate. Indeed, the parody is of the very notion of an original."[10]

Thoroughly bound within the confines of social law, we cannot abandon the idea of gender identity. Such ideas and identities (which are, as Butler reminds us, simply fantasies themselves) organize and make meaning of experience within the limits of cultural allowances. Encounters with other cultures are unsettling because they remind us that principles we take for granted, such as the idea that gender and anatomy are mutually identified, do not hold as cross-cultural constants. In many Native American tribes, for example, gender has been understood to be acquired and has not been so strictly dichotomized into male and female. Some individuals find themselves, through dreams or early inclinations, fitting neither traditional male nor female roles. They combine aspects of the two genders and constitute what can be understood as perhaps third and even fourth categories.[11] Such people are respected for their differences; often they are considered to be more powerful spiritually than other people.

Cultural allowances function on behalf of political dynamics, or as Flax says of gender, relationships of domination. Limits that provide organization and meaning to experience are not comfortably changed; power relations do not shift without great resistance. Nevertheless, someone at the edge is always pressing the limit further until new social law is generated. The more radical homosexual presses the limit of gender. Some have argued that the cultural fear of gender variation may be the bedrock of homophobia.[12] Radicals and conformists alike live to some extent within the same social rules, and those who defy, negate, or ignore these rules suffer individual penalties. People who try but inevitably fail to meet social requirements about gender (as everyone does to some degree) devise their own solutions and resolutions.

Sue Vargo has described the difficulties lesbians encounter in developing a positive identity in interaction with social expectations for women, which are inherently limiting, and social expectations of heterosexuality.

> Lesbians do not escape the major themes of female socialization in that as women we are trained to different degrees to be other-oriented, dependent, and passive rather than self-assertive. However, lesbians start at a different point in the process of resolving the conflict between being gender appropriate and having a positive self-image. Lesbians are already being seriously gender inappropriate in their sexual preference for other women. Their positive self-image cannot come only from gender appropriateness—it has to involve a positive valuing of gender inappropriateness if they are to value their lesbianism.[13]

A woman may feel confused about gender role identifications, she may feel isolated and fundamentally different from other women, or she may think of herself as having "male" traits, as being an "exceptional" woman, or as being crazy. "How individual lesbians resolve their self-image . . . varies immensely in terms of individual psychologies, norms of their immediate community be it heterosexual or gay, and their socioeconomic situations. Lesbians living in feminist and well-supported gay communities may arrive at a more radical vision of self that includes a positive sense of choosing a blend of so-called male and female behaviors for self."[14]

Gender Identities: Transitions and Ambiguities

There is in everyone some degree of identification with both parents which allows the child to embody both genders within the self, what Joyce McDougall terms as our psychic bisexuality, our wish to *be* as well as to possess the opposite-sexed parent.[15] Irene Fast proposes a model of gender development in which boys and girls gradually differentiate themselves out of an undifferentiated matrix. Before the differentiation period, "no aspect of maleness or femaleness is yet excluded."[16] Maleness and femaleness are not experienced as mutually exclusive categories; all sex and gender possibilities are available. At this primal level, one can embody maleness or femaleness without lacking the other.

As anatomical differences are observed, gender categories become differentiated. Masculinity and femininity become opposites, not merely in anatomy but also in behaviors and personal characteristics associated with them. This assignment of gender brings a profound sense of limitation:

> The meanings . . . include whatever the child ascribes to male-
> ness or femaleness. . . . For example, a girl may feel that without
> a penis she has nothing, no worthwhile genital organ. She may
> give up activity, adventurousness, and independence for passiv-
> ity and masochism, but these are not biological givens deter-
> mined by an actual, physical lack. Similarly a boy may believe
> that without the powerful creativity with which he invests
> childbearing, he is without creative power, and doomed to an
> empty and impersonal life. These are not, however, biological
> givens determined by his maleness. They are the meanings with
> which he has invested femaleness.[17]

This account, like other analytic perspectives, omits the crucial awareness
that culture has already determined much of this meaning, and the
child is gradually becoming acculturated through sorting out gender
"appropriateness." We may ask why it is necessary that anatomical
differences carry such psychological limitations. As Fast argues that
these limits are not imposed by biology, I would add that they are
imposed by psychology only in conjunction with cultural traditions
and social laws. Identifications with parents interact with other social
experiences to form one's consciously felt gender identity.

In the interviews, I asked women about family identifications and
where they felt their family alignments were. Their responses encompassed a wide range of identifications and disidentifications with
mothers, fathers, brothers, and sisters, which did not constitute
any kind of pattern. A number of women spoke of shifting identifications, from mother to father (or vice-versa) as they moved into
adolescence, reflecting that "history of identifications" to which Butler refers. Marty, who is bisexual, described the correspondence of
these shifts with family resemblances. Her account suggests the diversity of factors that determine identifications: genetics, social condi-
tioning, emotional bonding, and family needs and projections. She
also described a fluidity of identity that may be encountered in pieces,
corresponding to the postmodernist conception, and unlike the idea of
a unified and coherently enduring identity that many psychological
theories favor.

> I grew up as a tomboy. I think I was identified with my dad for a
> couple of reasons. My older sister looks like my mom a lot. I'm
> built very much like my dad, and I have his darker coloring. So I
> was sort of my father's daughter. Also my parents clearly wanted
> a son by the time I came along. By default I became the tomboy

for Dad. It feels like it suited me. I loved being outdoors and my sister didn't. But there were also lots of ways I got reinforced for it. So I was the one who went fishing with my dad and I really looked up to him. I'm still very close to my father. He's very nurturing. I admire and enjoy him.

But as I got older. . . . I'd always been close to my mother in another way. My mother is a very powerful personality, in good and bad ways, so our relationship was more ambivalent. She was very attached to me and protective of me. By the time I got to junior high, my face started looking more like my mother's, and I clearly enjoyed, as I became more feminine, a closer relationship with her. I identified more with her then than with my father.

In the responses to my question about identities and alignments within the subjects' families, I was struck by the fact that many of the women mentioned some way in which one or both parent seemed to be androgynous or to have switched roles. Sometimes women identified fathers as the nurturing one in the family, sometimes as the passive one while mothers were more instrumental or more authoritative. Often this was experienced as positive, a particular asset that other families lacked. In a few instances family life was described as unhappy, for example, when the mother was domineering and the father useless.

It seemed likely that many of these women unconsciously felt that they had been granted some flexibility about gender through their parents' more androgynous personalities. At the same time, some mentioned that their siblings were extremely traditional in their gender roles. What enables one child to find an opportunity for herself in a family trait while another reacts against it is something that defies consistent interpretation. Nevertheless, for the women I interviewed it seemed clear that parental variation was very important to a sense of gendered self.

Because people are diverse in the extent to which they identify with their own sex, lesbian and heterosexual women alike may experience themselves as masculine in important ways that have nothing to do with confusion about gender identity and may be either highly valued or felt as deviant.[18] Paula described the complex interaction that familial and social influences had upon her experience.

When I was first a lesbian I would have identified fiercely as a butch. That was less about sexuality and more about presenting a tough, armored image to the world. The message I got in my family was that a woman is not the thing to be. Period. I looked at my brother and my sister and saw how my parents treated them. If I had a choice here, clearly I would not choose to be a woman. So I think I had a tremendous identification with my brother and adopted a lot of his mannerisms. None of this was conscious at the time. It's only in hindsight that I can see it. Being "butch," being a construction worker, never wearing anything that would make me sexually appealing to men was really a big protection. It was also a way to say "I'm identifying with the power here." I mean I worked with them, I competed with them. That was my arena. Part of my process has been to soften a lot. Just what I wear has completely changed in the twelve years that I've been a lesbian. If I look what they would consider feminine now, it's okay.

Jan observed that others may not be able to understand the early experiences of women like herself who came out very young. "There's the whole area of gender and sex role differences which I don't think they get unless they manage to be straight and still be 'gender inappropriate.' If they always wanted to wear cute little ruffled petticoats and their grandmother gave them party shoes and they were happy because those things all go together with little girls. . . . then they don't get the pressure of being drawn to something they're not supposed to be drawn to, like always wanting to wear high-tops instead. They don't get all that lack of reinforcement."

Especially because of her adolescent experiences outside the mainstream of socialization processes, a primary lesbian may have a different experience of her gendered self than a girl who is involved with boys, who thinks of marrying, and who is typically feminine. It is untenable, however, to argue that the primary lesbian necessarily experiences herself as masculine or even androgynous, or that the bisexual lesbian necessarily feels herself to be more feminine. Some research suggests that most lesbians tend to be more androgynous than heterosexual women.[19] Other studies show a more highly developed sense of masculinity in lesbians than in heterosexual women, but simultaneously an equally developed sense of femininity in both groups.[20]

None of these studies distinguishes between these two groups of lesbians, so no conclusions can be drawn about whether some differences might be found. Nevertheless, the force of social experience, especially in adolescence, may leave lesbians who emerge early in life outside the usual sex-role socializing, a process that tends to affirm conventional gender stereotypes. Because early-developing lesbians have not played the part of an adolescent female in traditional ways, feelings about gender role identification may be more conflicted. This dimension is closely tied to that sense of self as deviant.

The larger question of what defines masculinity and what defines femininity is very much in flux culturally. Heterosexuals are confused about both role behavior and subjective sense of gendered self as these notions are rethought, and they challenge them in various ways. The studies that show lesbians to be more androgynously identified or, put another way, as embodying both traditionally masculine and feminine behaviors and attributes, suggest some flexibility in gender-related dimensions.

I could discern no patterns of differences in gender role identifications in the small sample of women I interviewed. Although some primary lesbians saw themselves as tending toward masculinity and some described themselves as more feminine, in one way or another all discussed the importance of both aspects of themselves. The bisexuals referred to themselves in similar ways; they tended first to speak of themselves as more feminine but almost immediately qualified this in some way. For example, Janine said, "I always thought of myself as feminine, and I come across that way—until I open my mouth. Then everyone finds out fast that I'm not what they expected."

A fundamental signifier of femininity in our culture, the desire to bear a child, did not distinguish the two groups. Three of the four bisexual women I interviewed individually had children from their heterosexual years. One of the primary lesbians had borne a child within a lesbian relationship, and another was considering doing so. Two of the four couples had children. Alix and Carol are raising Alix's two sons from her heterosexual marriage, sharing the parenting amicably with the children's father. Abby and Suzanne have an infant daughter, and Suzanne, the primary lesbian, is the birth mother.

The Significance of Gender in Lesbian Relationships

From the perspective of heterosexuality as an implicitly universal model of romance and eroticism, lesbian relationships, like male homosexual relationships, must be patterned in some way along gender lines. In this view, they rest entirely upon gender differences that reside in one partner's disturbed gender identification and the other's collusion in this impossible fantasy. In the terms of much of psychoanalytic and popular literature, there is the "butch," the pseudo-masculine lesbian who takes the part of the husband or male lover in both behavior and dress, and the "femme," who is not quite a true woman, being lesbian, but a caricature of femininity: helpless, narcissistic, hysterical, maternal, and wifely. Through their mimicry of heterosexual love, they may find some measure of satisfaction.

When the feminist movement challenged gender roles in heterosexual relationships, it simultaneously challenged this idea of lesbian couples. Many studies of lesbian relationships supported this challenge by demonstrating the rarity of role-playing.[21] Other studies found that lesbians are most satisfied in their relationships when they share power and decision-making with their partners, and when there is an absence of roles.[22] Some argue instead that heterosexual relationships are culturally determined by role-playing and perpetuate roles in constrictive ways.[23]

Still the concepts of butch and femme linger, often a matter of play and parody among lesbians as a shorthand way of addressing differences related to traditional gender conceptions, a kind of in-group joking that nevertheless carries real meaning. The women I interviewed all denied using or identifying with these terms, but many laughed and said, in one way or another, that they liked the idea of being a "butchy femme" or a "femmy butch."

Dina, a primary lesbian, spoke of the way she sees herself and her relationships in roles. "I always felt more identified as femme, although I think I actually come off as more butch. It's both really. I act competent, I'm defended. I emulated my two brothers. I thought it seemed like a better way to be in the world. But then in relationships I've always been more femme. Just ask my lovers! I like 'femmy butches,' and I think I'm a 'butchy femme.'" Abby, a bisexual, said, "I once saw a button that I bought because I liked that it described me as a butchy femme. I wore it for awhile. I'm always described as coming on like a Mac truck, but I'm definitely a femme."

One of the couples described themselves in much the same way.

JANINE: Butch and femme? Maybe those terms used to fit more. We've talked about this a lot. The difference is in how you talk and act. I present myself as a femme, but I am more butch. She's just the opposite. I think we like it that way.
KAREN: It's the way we play it out. . . . Well, I don't know if there's really much difference there, or if we think in those categories.
JANINE: We resist these categories, but I do think we fit them.
KAREN: I don't think it's really butch or femme because we're not at either end. It's kind of a gradation. Not polarities, but much closer to the center.

Lesbians cannot fail to be aware that in their choice of women as partners, and in the nontraditional life that accompanies this choice, they defy usual female roles. Thus I think there is always some interplay between masculinity and femininity in lesbianism, which is not the same as enacting gender roles in stereotypical ways. A broader context is needed to understand the metapsychological significance of gender and roles in lesbian relationships. Cultural determinations of gender expression are usually overlooked. What may be meaningful for particular reasons at a particular historical period may be misunderstood at later periods. As Jonathan Katz points out in his history of gay culture in American, "all homosexuality is situational, influenced and given meaning and character by its location in time and social space."[24]

The shift in meaning of gender dichotomy in lesbian relationships from the 1920s to the 1970s, for example, illustrates the necessity of this perspective. As Havelock Ellis drew it, the butch and the femme, rather than the primary or bisexual lesbian, dominated the popular conception of lesbian couples. During the 1920s lesbians first struggled for public recognition of the nature of their relationships. They were more concerned with establishing their relationships as sexual ones than with challenging the fundamental distortions of gender conceptions for heterosexual women as well as themselves. The approach of the sexologists was useful; it progressed beyond previous notions of relationships between women (as asexual) and argued that homosexuality was an inborn deviation of nature that must be tolerated.

Male homosexual identity was then a fairly recent construct, less than a century old. As Elizabeth Wilson points out, "The construction of lesbian identity appeared to be of even more recent origin, not gaining widespread recognition, in Britain at least, until *The Well of Loneliness* [an important early lesbian novel, see chapter 10] was prosecuted and banned in 1928. So it is not surprising that lesbians, emerging at the same time with a conscious identity, had, during these years, accepted the sexologists' definition of their 'condition' as biologically determined and clinical, one to which masculinity was the key."[25] Identifying as male was also, for these women, a progressive statement more about women's sexuality than about gender rules.[26]

By the 1970s the feminist and gay liberation movements could build upon these earlier gains and press the advance in a different direction. They could address the distortions required by gender rules and argue that women incorporate supposedly masculine attributes as women, not as men. Embracing a masculine identity was seen as questionable; it suggested a devaluation of women: "lesbianism now came to seem the escape route from the socially constructed gender roles imposed in a particularly rigid way on women. Paradoxically, the role-playing falsity of gender was, according to this scenario, the mark of heterosexuality, while lesbianism by contrast became the arena for the flowering of real womanhood."[27]

The shifting meanings of and attitude toward gender roles in lesbian relationships have continued to evolve as the feminist and lesbian movements have correspondingly changed. Many contemporary lesbians consider role-playing of a very fluid kind to be interesting, fun, and erotic. Wendy, the only woman I interviewed who felt that the complementarity in her relationship was primarily gender-based, described the shifts in her own attitudes and use of gender roles over the years, again revealing that "history of identities" that Butler's deconstructionist analysis describes.

> Over the years I've identified with the terms butch and femme in different ways. Initially it was kind of disgusting to me. After I came out, it was the first supportive niche I found. I tried to read everything written about lesbianism. I remember reading about role-playing and thinking it was very heterosexual. I didn't understand it except that it was sort of archaic, that it was the way it had been, and it wasn't like that anymore. That was the best I could understand it. After coming out and being a lesbian for awhile, I took a neutral stance. One of my first girlfriends identified as butch. I had very short hair then and didn't wear make-up or jewelry. I couldn't think of myself as butch exactly, but [laughs] I didn't like the idea of "femme," so it was hard to identify with either. I kept that stance for awhile. I remember when I started wearing make-up or earrings or whatever again, maybe I put on some lipstick. Everyone cheered, and they were saying, "Now we know she's a femme." But I didn't really accept that. Now I don't think about it much at all, but I think I would identify as a femme, whatever that means. Some women I've been with feel like they move back and forth, but they identify more as butch. You know, they pack the car and I pack the lunch. In the last couple of years I've been wearing skirts and [laughs] I even bought a real bra, not just a running bra. I've been with my lover for five years now, and we play around with it [role-playing]. It's fun. We're not role-bound, but we have an acceptance of those ideas [butch and femme], that they're okay, and that they're okay as sexual roles.

The underlying theme that emerged from my interviews was that gender is fluid and shifts over time and within the context of environment. A woman can use this fluidity both to find a place for herself in the world and to make her own statement. Even while she emphasizes one aspect of her sense of gender, another side hovers in the background, close to her awareness. In love relationships in particular, women draw upon this fluidity in ways that add interest, mystery, and sometimes tension to their intimacy.

Gender Devices
and Desires

9 | Most women I interviewed made some differentiation about gender between themselves and their partners. It seemed to me that here, perhaps more than with other aspects of complementarity, was ample room for projection. Because the partners in a lesbian couple may themselves have different conceptions of what each represents in gendered expression, they may use such expression according to personal interests and desires. As some have argued, "in same-sex couples . . . even small differences in the gender identities of the partners might lead them to play different gender roles."[1] This recalls again the concept of potential space, the psychological arena where partners put real or imagined differences to use. Through psychic play with intimacy and identity a new creation of self evolves.

The exchanges that take place provide a complementarity founded upon personal conceptions or even fantasies about gender rather than on actual gender-linked behavioral roles. A few writers point out that although stereotypical contemporary role-playing rarely exists, women have used role-playing in the coming-out process as a way to establish identity.[2] Others suggest that it exists as sexual play for some lesbians; such role-playing enhances sex but does not characterize other aspects of the relationship.[3] Heterosexual couples may similarly exaggerate gender roles to enhance sexuality. These interpretations suggest that role-playing is context-specific, a form of social communication rather than a consequence of intrapsychic confusion or conflict.

Differences in primary and bisexual lesbians' histories grant some leverage to the imagination; their relational tie is rich in projections of undeveloped parts of the self. The demands of gender conformity place so much constraint upon human development that unexpressed dimensions of the personality seek new opportunities to appear. In their relationships, primary and bisexual lesbians draw upon fantasies about what the partner, the "other" kind of lesbian, embodies.

A primary lesbian has gone through her adolescence and early adulthood outside of the usual feminine path. Perhaps, for example, male partners have not performed traditionally male tasks for her and she has depended upon herself in the arena of instrumental behavior. In this sense she has suffered less from the cultural devaluation of women and from restrictions on feminine behavior. At the same time she may be intrigued by—and desire to participate in—what is more clearly defined as the world of "the feminine."

A bisexual lesbian has been a party to that world, may have felt alienated within it, and yet may ·have embraced it. Through her relationships with men, she has been shaped to some extent by male expectations of feminine behavior. She may be more accomplished in or at ease with the traditional female world of emotionality. Wendy, for example, who has been married twice and raised a son, related that even in a lesbian relationship she automatically organizes the couple's social life and takes care of various social transactions. Her experience as a wife and mother make such actions second nature.

Correspondingly, a bisexual lesbian may have suffered from the cultural limitations imposed on her development because she is female. She may have internalized more of the cultural assessment, both positive and negative, of what it means to be female. Wendy was aware of these effects from her early experience; her reluctance to be identified as femme was directly related to her sense of the feminine as devalued. She also described her difficulties with more "masculine" things such as mechanical problems. She has little sense of identification with the masculine upon which to draw.

Complementarity around gender issues sometimes evolves in paradoxical ways. Alix related that her expression of femininity had changed in this, her first, lesbian relationship. She had been married for many years but always resisted expectations to dress and behave in typically feminine ways. Now that she was with a woman, she enjoyed dressing and acting in these same ways and with an ease and pleasure she had lacked. She would not be misunderstood here, she felt. She projected onto her lover Carol a familiarity with these aspects, which in fact Carol did not corroborate. At the same time, by appreciating certain previously neglected aspects of Carol, Alix encouraged her to also be more traditionally feminine. For Alix, the surprise of the relationship was a new freedom to explore femininity. She no longer worried about what she had always considered to be her more masculine qualities—

her aggressiveness and ambition—because she assumed they, too, would be appreciated.

Carol shifted in some ways as well. She dressed somewhat less androgynously (for example, she began wearing more jewelry) and felt she was more emotionally open than she had been before the relationship. As she described it, she had acquired a defensive emotional invulnerability in her early years as a lesbian, a protective armor against a world that did not value her as she was. Carol's attachment to this more "masculine" attitude had given way to a reevaluation, a greater desire to be expressive and responsive. At the same time, she felt highly appreciated for her lack of traditional female experience. She thought Alix tended to idealize her independence and autonomy. Carol's increased ambition in her work was through her participation in Alix's ambitiousness rather than through her own history of independence. In other words, she accepted at least some of her lover's projections and incorporated them into her own sense of self; she also returned some appreciation of these qualities, which allowed Alix to reown them in a new, less conflicted, way.

Projections of masculinity and femininity are evident on both sides of this relationship. Each woman found herself moving further in both directions through her perceptions of her lover. These were sometimes projections of self rather than accurate perceptions of the lover, an aspect of the relationship that was more or less conscious and sometimes mutually explored. Both women felt their differences in sexual experience, adolescent struggles, and sense of self as deviant. These dimensions were subject to discussion and accessible to consciousness in ways that other parts of complementary exchange (such as psychosexual organization) are not. How this complementarity is effected over time was expressed succinctly and metaphorically by another couple.

> KAREN: Our differences used to be greater. We've ended up balancing each other out more over the years.
> JANINE: You kind of sand each other down.
> KAREN [laughs]: Yeah, I decided to curl my hair.

When I asked Miriam, a bisexual, and Ellen, a primary lesbian, about gender roles, butch and femme, they revealed a shift in styles and a different interest in gender play.

> Q: Are butch and femme meaningful terms to you?
> ELLEN: We don't know what to do with them. Externally, to the world, our appearances suggest I'm butch, and Miriam is femme. However in our relationship, it's not so. In our sexual relationship,

the roles are probably reversed, although I don't quite know what butch and femme roles are sexually anyway. We share initiation, but I'd say Miriam is more in control. She is more controlling in general.

MIRIAM: It's true. It was a surprise. She thought it would be just the opposite when we first got together.

ELLEN: The women I'm attracted to tend to be more feminine. I'm not sure what's going on there. It may have to do with power and control, the illusion that I could be dominant [they look at each other and both laugh].

MIRIAM: I think we *both* look femme.

ELLEN: I'm not sure about that. But *you're* getting butcher. . . . I like it.

Q: Do you agree?

MIRIAM: No, I don't. I'm developing a style which is not so feminine, but it's not butch.

ELLEN: I think my style is developing into . . . femme's not the right word, but I've gotten more stylish.

MIRIAM: I love it when she's "femmed up." It's a real sexual turn-on.

ELLEN: Miriam would really like us both out in public in heels and nylons. There's a kinky aspect to that that she really likes.

MIRIAM: It's the idea of being physical with somebody who's really dressed like a woman. Then this is really lesbian! This is two women! I mean, pantyhose and everything! It's a real turn-on to me. The idea of being in a restaurant and sliding my hand under her skirt and over her silky pantyhose. Wow! [Both are laughing]. She can't get into it.

ELLEN: I hate pantyhose. However we're going to try it.

MIRIAM: She amenable. She's willing to explore my fantasy.

ELLEN: Heels, though, no way.

Another couple, Abby (bisexual) and Suzanne (primary lesbian), did not relate to the terms *butch* and *femme* at all. In terms of their appearance, Suzanne said, "We can both get very dressed up and be very feminine. We both started wearing make-up after we got together. We can both look like real jocks. We certainly don't use those categories in the way we relate, and we try not to use them sexually." However, they thought there was something like a gender difference in their emotional styles.

SUZANNE: I tend to have some real characteristic male tendencies around processing emotions and around social stuff. Like, you watch a woman and man go to a party and come back, and you find out that the woman will be able to tell you so much more about the people she's talked with. That's how Abby is. In the world, I have more masculine characteristics.

ABBY: It almost broke us up at the beginning of our relationship because she never asked me any questions. I'd tell her a story or something, and she'd just listen. She would never ask me to pursue anything. I began to think either she's not very deep, or she's not interested in me. I didn't know what the problem was. . . . When we got together five years ago she was just beginning to recognize that she had feelings and allow them. I remember saying to her "Oh, God. I'm going to have to go through years now of you learning what your feelings are, and then you're going to have to over-express them because that's what you have to do in the process of learning. And then the next stage is you have to figure out what you do when you don't get what you want." I was thinking I don't want to go through all that. I went through it ten years ago, and I didn't want to do it again. Thank God, she was a quick study.

Karen (a primary lesbian) and Janine (bisexual) remembered coping with a similar dichotomy, one stereotypically associated with male versus female behavior, in their early years.

JANINE: We had one date in the summer, and we had a terrible time. We went out to dinner together. She was upset about something, but she's very quiet. [They laugh.] She told me not to say that any more, but at that time, let's just say, she was not a major talker. She did not talk. She didn't tell me she was upset. Conversation was the most constipated effort. I walked away that night—I remember it very clearly—thinking there's absolutely no point in seeing this person any more because I can't talk to her. Eventually when we got involved, I said to her, I can't be involved with you if you don't talk to me. I can't not know what's going on. I've got to have a commitment to struggle with all this stuff. And she said she would, and we spent a long time getting through all that.

KAREN: But it worked. And then it fell into place. We put ourselves in a difficult situation and were able to come through it. One of the differences between us is that I think things through, all the way through. And do that ahead of time. Janine doesn't. That used to be a problem, but now she relies on me to do that [they laugh again], to tell her how she's going to feel about something when it happens. She was much more in the moment. I think that's one way we've turned a problem into a better thing. You even think about things more.

JANINE: Yes. But my basic m.o. is just to get to the situation and handle it when I get there. I'm often caught unaware by that. I'm much more impulsive than she is.

KAREN: We may be very much alike internally, but still we manifest ourselves differently in the world. Janine's more effusive, and I'm more calm, steadier. We're much more balanced now.

Reshaping Genders, Transcending Genders

Some writers have argued that feminism's antagonism to role-playing or lesbian expressions of gender differences denies homosexuality—its room for psychic play, its capacity for transformation and transcendence of gender.[4] Paula discussed the importance of such psychic play in her life.

> I love role stuff. This is one of the things I really love about being lesbian. I love switching roles. I find a lot of power in that. There are days I like to look really butch—wear a leather jacket and look tough. And there are days I like to wear make up and really "femme out." I really like both parts of myself and I feel like I have the most latitude to express them as a lesbian. And that's true sexually as well. I like the whole ball of wax. I think that's what's happened in the last twelve years. I've gone from a very narrow, frightened, protected place to having a much richer identity with a lot more latitude.

Elizabeth Wilson suggests that "normalizing" lesbianism by denying its use of gender play may itself be homophobic and that feminism has erred in the direction of a new moralism about sexual behavior that emphasizes relationship over sexuality, woman-identification and bonding over eroticized otherness. "I don't know, but I certainly never longed for 'the power of womanbonding.' That suggested something too maternal, too suffocating; I always wanted my lover to be *other*, not like me. I did not want to be bathed, drowned in the great tide of womanliness."[5] Homosexuality moves beyond either affirming or denying gender differences. Instead, in Wilson's analysis, it "destabilizes" our conception of gender by questioning gender's construction. This is the threat of homosexuality: "to insist on lesbianism as a challenge to stereotypes of gender is ultimately . . . political."[6] It points toward an alternative to insitutionalized relationships of domination.

The butch has certain psychological functions in the culture. The way she fails to fit in appears in two guises. In heterosexual and psychoanalytic literature, she is pitiable and unattractive, the woman who is not a woman. Sometimes, however, especially in lesbian literature and culture, she is the opposite: the strikingly handsome woman, lonely and aloof but desirable, romantic, and mysterious, the Byronesque figure that Radclyffe Hall, Colette, Djuna Barnes, and others depicted.[7] In the first guise, she carries cultural fears about failure to conform to gender rules. In the second, she holds the excitement of potentiality and freedom (sexual as well as gender), transcending its cost.

This second configuration keeps the butch a mythic figure in lesbian culture. The promise she carries makes lesbians not want to give her up, even where role-playing is not the currency of the culture. She is the figure of the man in the woman and the woman in the man. She suggests simultaneously the masterful mother and the nurturing father. She is a chance view of the underside of the psyche that is usually unseen. To know her is to be able to see into the shadows, to glimpse the dark side of the moon. The excitement of androgyny is in its possibilities for spying beneath the wraps of social rules.

The figure of the butch is a redefinition of what is feminine. Once we begin to dismantle the idea that there is something "essential" to masculinity or femininity, we can see these categories as ever-shifting and impossible to differentiate fully. For women, it may be more appropriate to speak of two differently developed versions of femininity rather than of masculinity versus femininity. Two of the women I interviewed broached this idea themselves. Jan, a primary lesbian, said, "It seems to me it's all layers. The more extremely feminine someone is the more aggressive and power-seeking she is, which brings her around to the other side. It just has to do with power and how you want to convey your sense of power to the world. Either extreme, you're trying really hard to do that, so it evens out in the end." Maggie, a bisexual, also thought both versions of the gender dichotomy should be called feminine when applied to women; they are simply two aspects of female experience.

Thinking of the feminine as a double-faceted experience is how one comes to understand lesbianism as woman-to-woman love rather than as disguised heterosexual pursuit. Each lover seeks the woman in her partner, but perhaps a woman different than herself. She seeks the nurturing woman, the masterful woman, or some less clearly dichotomized femininity in her lover, and to know it in herself, in her own grasp of what it is to be female.

This idea does not complete the picture; it simply expresses what is usually omitted or denied in it. A gay woman may also have an interest in what is male and wish to incorporate the male in some aspect into her life and relationship. Her interest can be a desire to find what is male in a way that does not negate what is female. Efforts to drain lesbian (or gay male) attractions of gender-related meaning risk denying the reality that the sexes each manifest themselves in some way, however culturally constructed. Psychoanalysis has sometimes argued that homosexuality is founded on such unconscious denial.[8] Instead, lesbianism may be understood to incorporate awareness, both conscious and unconscious, of gender in a different way. This way *may* be through the medium of consciously expressed gender identifications, but this is not the only possibility.

An analysis of lesbian relationships founded upon differences in orientation of sexual desire reveals another medium, the unconscious recognition of sex differences. The male is present in absentia, not in denial; each woman's relationship to heterosexuality carries this meaning. In heterosexual relationships, homosexual expression is found in absentia through projective identification or vicarious experience of the other's role as partner to a man or woman (chapter 11). In lesbian relationships, through unconscious psychosexual exchanges, the male as a potential but not actualized erotic partner may also be present in absentia.

The need for the male to be present only in absentia is a consequence of the painful conditions of gender relations. For many lesbians, the choice of another woman as a partner expresses at some level a deep desire not to suffer the usual constrictions of femininity that heterosexuality mandates. It is paradoxically a desire to seek a fuller expression of being female, of femininity within herself. The alternative woman, who spans both ends of the gender continuum, exists only in the absence of the male. Her lineage goes back to the Greek mythic expression of women who disavowed marriage and heterosexuality: Athena, Artemis, and Atalanta.[9] Like them, like the "marriage resisters" in China, like women elsewhere who chose to remain single even when the social cost is high, the lesbian seeks to bring herself into being in a way that seems, sadly, only to be possible in the absence of the male.[10]

Conclusion

There is usually an unconscious (and occasionally conscious) oscillation of gender dimensions in lesbian relationships. At times gender play is found along the lines of a masculine-feminine complementary interaction; at other times it seeks an exploration of a feminine-feminine connection. Perhaps there is even a symbolic masculine-masculine exchange. Not all couples participate in these interactions, and couples that do, participate to different degrees. While all couples can engage in such exchange, perhaps homosexual relationships have both a greater freedom and a greater desire to do so in what are sometimes fairly conscious ways.

The earlier discussion of relational processes suggested that an important aspect of heterosexual relationships is the potential for projected and introjected elements of masculinity and femininity between the man and woman.[11] These strengthen the individual's gender identity: "feminine wishes in the man and masculine wishes in the woman are projected onto the partner, enhancing one's own gender identity and therefore the boundaries of the self."[12] This exchange may be more important to heterosexual relationships, which confirm a place within a social institution based upon entrenched gender differences. Between lesbians, gender exchanges may expand women's sense of gender, not confirm it. The alternative is possible in heterosexual relationships too, of course, but it may be more threatening there.

Ironically, lesbians and gay men are not necessarily those most oppressed by gender rules and constraints; perhaps they are even the least oppressed, while traditional women are the most. Lesbians carry conscious knowledge of oppression by gender rules that they experience through their deviation from them. More traditional women may give little thought to gender rules, but then embody the limitations of them in their lives. What lesbians gain from their burden of awareness is greater degrees of freedom within their own experiences of self and gender.

Gender-deviant lesbians may not be seeking to escape from the constraints of femininity into masculinity, or even into androgyny, although that is how many express it. Instead, they may be striving for an escape from the limitations of gender categories into something more variable and fluid, a transcendance of gender rules altogether. Any form of complementarity that oscillates around variations and alterations in gender roles or rules in lesbian relationships permits a degree of this transcendance.

Literary Illusions

10 The distinction between primary and bisexually oriented lesbians may be more fundamental than one based upon gender identifications. Either is a theoretical construction however. Neither represents discrete categories, but rather the ends of a continuum. As the Kinsey studies showed, sexual orientation varies from the extremes of exclusive homosexual or heterosexual inclination to many in-between degrees of interest.[1] Likewise, gender identification is relative, and a purely masculine or feminine identification is a theoretical construct rather than an actuality.

Complementarity founded upon differences in sexual orientation is not always the basis of lesbian relationships—other forms of complementarity certainly exist. In some relationships complementarity is based primarily upon subjectively felt differences in gender identification that may or may not be translated into role behavior. However, such complementarity has historically been given much credit that may, on closer examination, belong to differences in sexual orientation. Earlier chapters referred to the influence of the early sexologists, especially Krafft-Ebing and Havelock Ellis, on the traditionally understood complementarity of homosexuality as gender-based.

Ellis's portrayal of two kinds of lesbians who are drawn to each other is worth quoting at length because it was so influential and because it bears reanalysis.

A class in which homosexuality, while fairly distinct, is only slightly marked, is formed by the women to whom the actively inverted woman is most attracted. These women differ, in the first place, from the normal, or average, woman in that they are not repelled or disgusted by the lover-like advances from persons of their own sex. They are not usually attractive to the average man, though to this rule there are many exceptions. Their faces may be plain or ill-made, but not seldom they possess good figures: a point which is apt to carry more weight with the inverted woman than beauty of face. Their sexual impulses are seldom well-marked, but they are of strongly affectionate nature. . . . [T]hey are always womanly. One may perhaps say that they are the pick of the women whom the average man would pass by. No doubt, this is often the reason why they are open to homosexual advances, but I do not think it is the sole reason. So far as they may be said to constitute a class, they seem to possess a genuine, though not precisely sexual preference for women over men, and it is this coldness rather than lack of charm, which often render men rather indifferent to them.

The actively inverted woman usually differs from the woman of the class just mentioned in one fairly essential character: a more or less distinct trace of masculinity. She may not be, and frequently is not, what would be called a "mannish" woman, for the latter may imitate men on grounds of taste and habit unconnected with sexual perversion, while in the inverted woman the masculine traits are part of an organic instinct which she by no means always wishes to accentuate. The inverted woman's masculine element may, in the least degree, consist only in the fact that she makes advances to the woman to whom she is attracted and treats all men in a cool, direct manner, which may not exclude comradeship, but which excludes every sexual relationship, whether of passion or merely of coquetry. Usually the inverted woman feels absolute indifference toward men, and not seldom repulsion. And this feeling, as a rule, is instinctively reciprocated by men.[2]

This depiction of lesbian partner-choice became a standard view of masculine-feminine connection, or role-playing, that many writers adopted, both psychoanalysts and authors of homosexual material in journals and books for the lay public. A close look at its content reveals slim evidence of masculinity or femininity in either partner. Lack of interest in men seems to be the common element, not unexpectedly. In the latter case there is a clear lesbian choice, while in the former it is either more vaguely defined or more passively received, even by default. The masculine-feminine distinction seems to rest upon this active-passive dimension.

Ellis's distinction between the two kinds of lesbians is not based on gender identifications at all, and most of his subjects were not masculine in conventional terms.[3] His distinction actually rests upon another difference: what he terms the "true invert," who is inevitably lesbian, and the woman who is lesbian for lack of a better choice. The lesbian by default is "normal" and might accept a relationship with a man were she offered one. While making this distinction Ellis ignored both the economic necessity of marriage for most women and the fact that many women of this second category had fled marriages to be involved with women.[4] Thus heterosexuality may have been a matter of default not choice.

What sets this group of women apart from other lesbians is their participation at some point in relationships with men. Ellis's distinction is really the same that I make between primary and bisexual lesbians. He does not explore the meaning of this difference further but relies upon a superficial assignment of gender attributes, such as passive versus active, to account for it.

Ellis's work is largely responsible for the dissemination of stereotypes that still persist.[5] These ideas became a powerful repressive force against lesbian relationships and against deviant sex-role behavior of women in general.[6] Echoes of Ellis's ideas persisted in popular sensationalized novels and confessional magazines for decades. It is difficult to find any lesbian novel written before the 1960s that does not take his ideas as a given.

Ellis continually equated lesbianism and transvestism. Ironically, by openly cross-dressing, some women used his conceptions of lesbian relationships to establish the sexual nature of their relationships with other women. Esther Newton theorizes that beginning in the 1920s, many women chose to dress in men's clothes, as Ellis argued that lesbians did, in order to announce their sexuality more or less publicly.[7] The marginal social respectability of "Boston marriages" in the United States and in Victorian England had depended upon the tacit understanding that the couples involved, like most women, had little interest in sex. But by the 1920s, "To become avowedly sexual, the New Woman had to enter the male world, either as a heterosexual on male terms (a flapper) or as—or with—a lesbian in male body drag (a butch)."[8] The expatriate culture of Paris during the 1920s included a group of literary and artistic women, such as Radclyffe Hall, Natalie Barney, and Renee Vivien, who were famous for cross-dressing in public and proclaiming sexual liberation for lesbians. To abstract this sexual behavior entirely from its cultural context would conceal its full meaning. That is, to give it a purely psychological interpretation, such as disturbance in gender identity, would distort the internal and external realities of these women.

Psychoanalysts in the 1940s and 1950s continued to disseminate these ideas and to insist that such social manifestations of lesbian relations were nothing other than a consequence of severe intrapsychic disturbance.[9] According to them, lesbian relationships commonly involve role-playing that mimics heterosexual relationships. Some lesbian writers described role-playing from the 1930s to the 1950s, but pointed out that even then roles might be interchanged.[10] Phillip Blumstein and Pepper Schwartz have interpreted the rise and decline of role-playing among gay couples.

> It is our impression that homosexual couples went through the familial fifties right along with the rest of the country. At a time when traditional assumptions about sex roles in marriage remained unchallenged (husband as protector and provider, wife as homemaker and nurturer), many gay and lesbian couples fell into a pattern of role playing. . . . How prominent or widespread these patterns were among lesbians and gay men in the 1950's and earlier is impossible for us to know because of the lack of research, but it is probably true that they were more common when gender roles were more rigidly adhered to by everyone.[11]

These observations suggest that roles represented complex social communication more than they did structured intrapsychic development. The enormous influence of the early sex studies is apparent on both psychoanalytic and popular portrayals of lesbian couples. A novel from this period shows the literary influence of Ellis's work and illustrates again how one view may conceal the other.

The Well of Loneliness

The classic lesbian novel *The Well of Loneliness*, by Radclyffe Hall created a sensation when it was published in 1928, receiving the ultimate recognition of being banned in England for many years (and for a short while in the United States). It continues to be reprinted and read, many years after its initial publication. *The Well* is unlike the pulp novels about lesbians (which until the 1970s and 1980s were the only popular literature on lesbianism) in that its author had serious artistic intentions as well as the desire to bring the subject of homosexuality before the public. Although it strikes the modern reader as being mired in post-Victorian sentiment and style, the book was widely praised in its time as both an admirable literary work and a "daring and heroic" one.[12] During the various court cases against it, many prominent writers came to the novel's defense, including T. S. Eliot, E. M. Forster, Julian Huxley, Lytton Strachey, and Virginia Woolf.

The first edition of Havelock Ellis's *Sexual Inversion* had appeared thirty years before Hall's work. Radclyffe Hall met Ellis, visited with him on several occasions, and acknowledged his influence upon her work.[13] His brief commentary on the novel was included in its first edition and subsequent others.

> I have read *The Well of Loneliness* with great interest because — apart from its fine qualities as a novel by a writer of accomplished art — it possesses a notable psychological and sociological significance. So far as I know, it is the first English novel which presents, in a completely faithful and uncompromising form, one particular aspect of sexual life as it exists among us today. The relation of certain people — who, while different from their fellow human beings, are sometimes of the highest character and the finest aptitudes — to the often hostile society in which they move, presents difficult and unsolved problems. The poignant situations which thus arise are here set forth so vividly, and yet with such complete absence of offence, that we must place Radclyffe Hall's book on a high level of distinction.[14]

Nevertheless, unlike others, Ellis refused to lend his name to the book's defense once it was under attack. Hall's biographer, Lovat Dickson, suggests that the explanation for both Ellis's interest and his ambivalence is that Ellis's wife had affairs with other women, with his knowledge.[15] He failed to defend even his own book publicly.

The book tells the story of lesbianism and lesbian relationships from the perspective of gender variation; the "true invert" is a trick of nature, an individual with the body of one sex and the soul of the other. Analysis of the novel shows how thoroughly interpretations based on gender may conceal the significance of sexual orientation. The heroine of *The Well of Loneliness* is Stephen Gordon, an upper-class British woman who begins to discover her inversion (as Hall always refers to it) when she is repulsed by a marriage proposal from Martin, a man she likes and admires. Before this realization is fully achieved, she knows only how different she is from other girls. She looks, dresses, and behaves like a boy and is utterly dismayed by the trappings of femininity. Her masculinity is overdetermined in the novel, as her name suggests. She is a born invert, masculine by nature and boyish even as an infant ("a narrow-hipped, wide-shouldered little tadpole of a baby"). She resembles her father in every way. At the same time, her father, determined to have a son, names her Stephen in spite of her sex. He encourages her masculine pursuits and protects her from her mother's efforts to feminize her.

Stephen's ultra-feminine mother is antagonized and repelled by her daughter's masculinity. In the face of maternal rejection, little Stephen turns toward the housemaid, whom she pursues and courts in belated oedipal fashion at age seven. Her identification with her father is idealized throughout childhood and adolescence, and she wins his admiration through her skills in hunting and fencing. Thus Stephen's inversion is given not only as congenital, but also as reinforced by the family's dynamics.

The father realizes Stephen's inversion while she is still an adolescent. He reads Krafft-Ebing and other sexologists and recognizes his daughter in their descriptions. After he is dead, however, his protection is gone. When the mother discovers the nature of her daughter's sexuality through a letter from the husband of a neighbor with whom Stephen has been having an unconsummated affair, she exiles her from the family home. Stephen moves to London, becomes a well-known writer, and relinquishes hope of love and family. Eventually she moves to Paris but remains on the periphery of a circle of lesbian artists and writers.

When war is declared in 1914, Stephen goes to the front to serve with a women's ambulance corps. There she meets Mary Llewellyn, a young, innocent, and thoroughly feminine woman who eventually becomes her lover and companion. They live together in Paris after the war and are happy for a number of years. Through their circle of friends, readers are introduced to other lesbians and their relationships. Invariably the couples include a masculine-identified woman and her feminine lover; for the most part they are described as freakish and disturbed, at the very least unhappy. Their suffering is a combination of nature (the "nerves of the invert") and social persecution. Although the novel intends to be a sympathetic portrayal of homosexuality, it is also careful to uphold the moral expectations of its era. The lives of the homosexual characters are at best ones of brave isolation and at worst destroyed by suicide, alcoholism, or drug addiction. They are, as Elizabeth Wilson observes, "the haunted, the tormented, and the damned"—female Byronic figures.[16]

Ultimately Stephen realizes that this life is taking a great toll on Mary, who is "normal" except for her love of Stephen. Stephen's early suitor, Martin, reappears, this time to fall in love with Mary, whom he realizes has the capacity to return his love. In order to spare her from the suffering of a life as a social exile, Stephen sacrifices her own happiness and sends Mary into Martin's arms. The book closes with a plea to God and the world: "We have not denied You, then rise up and defend us. Acknowledge us, oh God, before the whole world. Give us also the right to our existence!"

The book was a courageous effort to bring homosexuality into the open and establish it as a variation of nature to be respected and expressed. At the same time, Hall carefully refrains from challenging stereotypes of lesbianism; through its worldwide attention her book disseminated them far more widely than Ellis's work alone could have. Hall argues for lesbianism to be tolerated, with all of its obvious pathology. Her plea for acceptance is ultimately founded upon pity more than respect. Buffy Dunker has noted, "Those of us who read Radclyffe Hall's *The Well of Loneliness* in the thirties were convinced that loving a woman meant taking on a man's role and would lead to misery and death."[17] The novel continues to be read, and it influences women, often as part of the rite of passage in coming out. A number of women in Julia Stanley and Susan Wolfe's collection of lesbian coming-out stories recall encounters with the novel as their introduction to lesbian life.[18]

According to Dickson, the novel is a semiautobiographical account of Hall's own life, with some romanticized additions to her family background. She was indeed a widely praised author in London in the 1920s. An earlier novel, *The Unlit Lamp*, was critically acclaimed, and *Adam's Breed* received the two highest literary prizes in Britain in 1926. Only E. M. Forster's *A Passage to India* had achieved such a distinction. Hall was prominent in literary circles in both London and Paris, part of the Parisian group of lesbian artists and writers that defied social constrictions by cross-dressing. As Esther Newton argues, this masculine expression drew upon Ellis's account of what a "real lesbian" was like and used his work to establish the women's sexuality in public terms.[19]

A View Hidden from View

Hall's understanding of lesbianism is dependent upon complementarity through gender differentiation, parallelling Ellis's ideas. In this analysis, a lesbian's inherent masculinity proves that her inversion is a product of nature. Being a man at heart she is inevitably attracted to women who are feminine, not to others like herself. Like Mary in the novel, such women are themselves "normal" except for the accident of their attraction to an inverted woman. The attraction takes hold because of the invert's masculinity.

Hall's own identity as both masculine and lesbian had emerged as early as adolescence. Although her given name was Marguerite Radclyffe Hall, she began calling herself John by her early twenties. She was often described as a handsome, rather than beautiful, woman. The most important relationship of her life was her partnership with Una Troubridge, her lover and companion from 1915 until Hall's death in 1943. Like most of the other women with whom Hall was involved, Troubridge was both beautiful and typically feminine. Also like the others, she was previously heterosexual. She was married to Admiral Troubridge, well-known for his naval exploits, and had one child, a daughter, when she was first attracted to Hall. Soon afterward Hall and Troubridge became involved and bonded deeply. From that point on, Troubridge refused to return to her husband's naval post, and within a few years the couple were legally separated.

Troubridge differed from Radclyffe Hall in her presumably bisexual inclinations perhaps more than simply in femininity. If Hall's manner and style of dress imputed masculininty, then Troubridge's must also be questioned. A portrait of her in the 1920s, during that period of more public lesbian declaration, shows Troubridge also wearing men's clothes. When she and Hall were confirmed in the Catholic church, they both chose male saints' names, to the priest's dismay. These details suggest that a masculine posture was at least to some extent intended as a cultural statement. More important, all of Hall's lovers were women who also had heterosexual inclinations. Hall's most significant relationship before Troubridge was with Mabel Batten, another married woman, a "well-known beauty of the time" and a patron of the arts who first took an interest in Hall's work.[20] It was only at Batten's death that Hall and Troubridge became lovers. Hall also had an important love affair toward the end of her life with Evgenia Souline, who later married. We can wonder whether this difference between Hall, the primary lesbian, and her lovers, more bisexually inclined, was not at least as significant as their gender-related differences.

An analysis of the novel's ending also lends itself to reinterpretation. Stephen becomes aware of Martin's love for Mary and Mary's potential for returning his love. She is at first combative. She and Martin agree to fight for Mary without Mary's knowledge. After a period of time they both know that Mary will never give up Stephen for Martin, and Martin prepares to leave Paris. This is the turning point for Stephen, as she realizes Mary will no longer have the chance for marriage and family:

And now she [Stephen] must pay very dearly indeed for that inherent respect of the normal which nothing had ever been able to destroy, not even the long years of persecution. . . . She must pay for the instinct which, in earliest childhood, had made her feel something akin to worship for the perfect thing which she had divined in the love that existed between her parents. Never before had she seen so clearly all that was lacking to Mary Llewellyn, all that would pass from her faltering grasp, perhaps never to return, with the passing of Martin—children, a home that the world would respect, ties of affection that the world would hold sacred, the blessed security, and the peace of being released from the world's persecution. . . . Only one gift could she offer to love, to Mary, and that was the gift of Martin.[21]

Stephen sacrifices her own happiness by impelling Mary to leave her for Martin; she professes not to love Mary any more. This passage and Stephen's actions may be viewed as an unconscious identification with Mary's heterosexuality. Like Anna Freud's description of altruistic surrender, Stephen gives Mary a life of acceptance, family, and friends, things Stephen herself abandons forever. Through a profound love for and identification with Mary, Stephen sends her into the other world that a life with Martin signifies.

This self-sacrifice (which strikes me as more stereotypically feminine than masculine in nature) suggests that Stephen makes an unconscious connection with her own potential for heterosexuality by sending Mary, against her wishes, to her own former suitor. Although Stephen does not wish to follow that route herself, neither can she foreclose it altogether. Through Mary she acknowledges "the instinct" that led her to idealize her parents' love. She also recognizes her "inherent respect of the normal." Mary is Stephen's connection with the dominant culture that she has renounced and been renounced by. To keep Mary in her world would close that door psychologically for both Stephen and Mary.

What this interpretation of Hall's novel suggests is that the cultural naming of complementarity in lesbian couples as masculinity related to femininity foreordained future analyses of lesbian relationships along the same lines. The popularity of Hall's work obscured other levels of complementarity that may lie even deeper in the psyche. What began as a descriptive account became fixed and ultimately prescriptive, determining the nature of lesbian relationships even for lesbians. For decades afterward, popular novels followed the pattern of The Well of Loneliness, becoming formula stories of lesbian love, contemporary reeditions in the terms of Hall's book. A stock character was a masculine, or butch, lesbian who encounters a series of *tres femme* lovers, and their love was always doomed to a bad end. When these affairs finally fail, usually the femme lover turns or returns to a man.[22] The gender polarity created an erotic charge with familiar associations. Other kinds of eroticism, a more female-to-female eroticism in particular, remained unthinkable.

As long as this gender overlay was a cultural and literary requirement, other aspects of lesbian lovers were obscured. Again, it is easy to equate primary lesbians with the figure of the butch and bisexual lesbians with the femme, but it is not necessarily accurate to do so. The illusion of fixed gender roles holds an appeal simply for its explanatory potential, but when these two aspects are separated, as I think they need to be, a multidimensional picture emerges of variation and play with gender and the meaning of gender. We can then begin to think about what other elements provide attraction, sustain interest, and become ties between women.

Three | Re-Viewing Traditional Views

The Rest
of the World
in Love

11 | What can be said about complementarity in lesbian relationships that are not based on a primary-bisexual match? What can we understand about heterosexual relationships from this lesbian perspective? If the ideas presented here describe intrapsychic and interpersonal exchanges that attract and bond lesbians, how do we understand lesbian relationships that do not fit this pattern? The question has several answers. The theory is not intended to be exhaustive; it explores the dynamics of complementary relating in certain lesbian couples and is also intended as a conceptual paradigm for the mechanisms of attraction and bonding that apply to many relationships. For other relationships the nature of exchange will be different, and in some cases, no doubt, highly idiosyncratic.

For some lesbians, the need to consolidate sexual identity may be paramount. Finding a partner with a similar psychosexual history can be an overriding concern. The relationship mirrors the experience of each rather than expresses an alternative. Two women who have both been married for a lengthy period can feel confirmed by each other's choice when they become involved. Conversely, two women who are both primary lesbians find affirmation of themselves most clearly in each other's history. At the same time, perhaps other dimensions of difference exist between them that are compelling. Ethel Person argues that "The longing in love is almost always across a perceived difference. . . . Perhaps the need for difference as the inspiration for love is nowhere better illustrated than among some male homosexuals. No longer having easy recourse to a difference grounded in biological sex, it is quite extraordinary how many homosexual lovers choose the love object across striking differences in age, culture, background, and general abilities and interests."[1] Person's observation is a casual one. It would be useful to know to what extent male couples actually do involve greater individual differences than heterosexual couples and whether lesbian couples also show a higher incidence of "striking differences." Further research about gay relationships is needed in this area.

Others contend, however, that differences are not necessarily the source of attraction between individuals. John Money argues that a partner must match one's "idealized and highly idiosyncratic image," and that "it is irrelevant whether the two partners are replicas or polar opposites of one another in temperament, interests, achievements, or whatever. What counts it that they fulfill each the other's ideal in imagery and expectancy."[2] Referring to heterosexual bonding, Bernard Murstein observes that narcissism may underlie object choice: "An older individual may love a younger person who seems to represent the qualities that the former possessed in his youth. A person may love another who represents what he would like to be."[3] Christine Downing describes gay people as "those of us who direct our love and sexuality primarily to others like ourselves, who have become who we are primarily through relationships based on analogy rather than contrast, on mirroring rather than the complementation of opposites."[4] Clearly, some people do not believe attraction comes through difference.

Surely both positions express some truth. Both sameness and difference hold a fascination. We are drawn to those who seem to be like us, who are a "double" of some kind, but clearly we are also intrigued with difference and how another person can be fundamentally different. We try to understand and encompass that difference by joining it. This double-play creates a powerful attraction, finding the difference within the sameness and the sameness within the difference.

To be complementary, a bond based upon differences must have some dimension of personal significance to the self. Issues of sexual orientation may or may not reflect such individual significance. For some women, differences in gender role identity *are* the essential attraction in their relationships. Even when differences in sexual orientation represent a meaningful dimension, they may be more threatening than appealing. A bisexual history or orientation can indicate a continuing interest in men as potential partners. Lesbians who come out after heterosexual relationships sometimes return to heterosexuality later. A primary lesbian may choose to protect herself from this possibility.

Lesbians whose orientation is more bisexual are aware that their bisexuality is sometimes not welcomed by other lesbians. Often, an underlying bisexual orientation is not acknowledged openly. When it is acknowledged, it is frequently criticized by other lesbians.[5] Carla Golden has noted this pressure for homogeneity in her survey of college students.

> The women with whom I spoke were not personally distressed by the fact of discrepancies between sexual behavior and sexual identity. For example, women who identified as lesbians but found themselves to be occasionally sexually attracted to men were made more uncomfortable by the thought of what other lesbians might think than by their own fluid and changing attractions. . . . Although very often they felt compelled to identify themselves publicly and unequivocally as lesbians whose sexuality was stable and enduring and exclusively focused on women, they privately experienced their sexuality in a more fluid and dynamic manner.[6]

Primary lesbians in Golden's survey sometimes implied that "elective" lesbians were "fake" lesbians. Clearly, tension between the two positions alienates as well as attracts, both in intimate relationships and within the community of lesbians. Internal conflicts about sexual orientation easily become external conflicts. Differences here may be suppressed, especially when consolidating one's identity is a developmental priority.

The lesbian liberation movement has gone through a period in which differences of many kinds, sexual orientation, politics, social values, and appearance, were resisted. Susan Krieger's work exploring lesbian communities during the 1970s described the pull for merger on a community level, similar to the pull for fusion between a couple.[7] The struggle to create a haven for lesbians and a united front against an often-hostile heterosexual culture overrode considerations of complex individual dissimilarities. Currently, tolerance of diversity and affirmation of differences seem to be emerging as communal values.[8] This may be a move toward differentiation after merger has reached its peak.

This book is in some ways a consequence of this change. Because differences in sexual interests were often denied by women with lesbian identities, this territory was not really accessible to observation. With some regularity, women "rewrote" their own histories, declaring their former relationships with men meaningless.[9] In many cases, this recasting of personal experience was authentic—certainly women are channeled into heterosexual relationships regardless of their inclinations—but it is difficult to know how much revision took place under the sway of subtle community pressures. Now that there is greater openness about diversity, real differences in orientation are more apparent. The past tendency to obscure such differences is surely one explanation for the scarcity of information about them.

Aside from defensive reactions, other women may view differences in sexual orientation as not holding much personal significance. If developmental needs are significant in partner choice, surely these needs will vary from woman to woman. Some choices may be more determined by identity requirements; for others, conscious and unconscious concerns about sexual orientation may have played themselves out sufficiently in former relationships and another kind of complementary bond is of more interest.

Even in a relationship founded on dissimilarity of sexual experience, its meaning may have been integrated, and with the passage of time other aspects of the relationship are significant. Relationships have their own developmental history. The vitality of a relationship is determined to some extent by its capacity to continue providing new territory for individual development.

The paradigm of complementarity is that of meaningful conscious and unconscious exchange through projective and introjective identification between the partners. The terms of this exchange can vary significantly. As a vehicle of complementarity, this process is universal, yet its content varies, in major and minor ways, with individual psychological needs and cultural allowances. Other analyses of relationships might highlight the ways in which class, racial, and cultural differences are also negotiated through this process. Intimate relationships rely upon projective and introjective exchanges, as do family relationships, social, and political ones. Whether these exchanges create satisfying alliances, promote growth, or generate destructive animosities is a matter of the meaning and purpose they hold in the psyche.

A common (perhaps universal) dimension of complementarity is the interchange of parent-child roles, that is, Freud's explanation of adult choices as always replicating in some sense the first object of love, a re-finding of some aspect of love for one's parents. We are most likely to be aware of this re-finding when confronting its negative aspect; we discover that what we disliked most in our parents is replicated in some way in our lover. A woman I interviewed said, "I think we're together because I act just like her mother, and she acts just like mine, at our worst." Some strands of such complementarity are found interwoven with every other possible dimension. Just as the dimensions of exchange I have explored here have not been readily apparent from previous analyses of lesbian relating, surely other dimensions will emerge as well. As theory about lesbian development grows, the dynamics of lesbian relationships will also be seen in new ways. This is a pursuit long-delayed, and further empirical, theoretical, and clinical study is necessary before the design takes shape.

The impact of differences in sexual history and identity may apply to relationships between gay men as well as lesbians. Certainly some developmental experiences described for lesbians are paralleled in early, adolescent, and adult experiences of gay men. A self-image as deviant, gender-identity concerns, and oedipal differences may be equally salient in male homosexuality. It seems wise to be cautious about drawing simple parallels between men and women, however. The differences in male and female development impart distinct differences in relationships. Some have argued that male sexuality is not as fluid as women's sexuality, that bisexuality is not as common to men as to women.[10] In this case, there is less ground for such complementarity to develop. Just as studies of male homosexuality do not always apply to lesbianism, dynamics of lesbian relationships may not fit gay male couples, either. Explorations of the characteristics of each are needed.

Heterosexual Relationships

At the beginning of this book I suggested that looking at heterosexual relationships from the viewpoint of homosexual ones could be an interesting pursuit. When heterosexuality is not taken as normative, one may see dynamic patterns not visible otherwise. Here, I will recapitulate and expand upon some of these perceptions. The primary reversal is to see the homosexuality latent in heterosexuality, corresponding to the heterosexuality latent in homosexuality. A similar kind of psychosexual exchange takes place at the unconscious (and sometimes conscious) level of experience. Some authors have pointed in a similar direction. Robert Knight, for example, observes that in heterosexual relationships, the man "projects onto [his lover] his own femininity and his own wishes and then tries to live up to them. . . . Reintrojection of this new object then occurs. The growing together and becoming alike of a man and woman in love with each other involves considerable interaction of projection and introjection, with resulting identification with each other."[11] In a similar vein, Murstein thinks that a woman "may be drawn to a man for the boyish qualities she herself possessed before she had to abandon them for 'girl's' behavior."[12]

In traditional formulations a gendered complementarity is effected between men and women. The man provides access to the external world of instrumentality, while the woman provides access to the internal world of emotions.[13] These informal observations implicitly reinforce the idea that all individuals search for experiences that allow unconscious access to a bi-gender potentiality.

It seems to me that other levels of exchange operate here as well. Each partner may experience his or her disowned homosexuality through a projection of self onto the partner. During emotional intimacy and love-making, moments of intense merger and identification occur. As a man identifies with the woman with whom he makes love, he knows something of what it is like to make love with a man. Part of his pleasure in love-making is to experience her pleasure vicariously through projective identification. For a moment, he is both the woman-in-the-man and the man-in-the-woman. As he imagines what it is like to feel a man's body so intimately, he partakes of the joys of same-sex love, even within opposite-sex love.

Likewise, the woman identifies with the man in love-making. She imagines, perhaps entirely unconsciously, what a woman's body is like to the one who is aroused by it. She takes pleasure in another's pleasure in her own body. She is both woman and man in this intimacy, and in that instance she knows something of what making love with a woman is like. As the woman projects herself into the man making love to her, she is both lesbian and heterosexual lover.

In a short story, Lorrie Moore expresses the identification that may occur between heterosexual lovers. For the protagonist, this identification becomes conscious in moments of jealous despair: "She had, without realizing it at the time, learned to follow his gaze, learned to know his lust, and . . . his desires remained memorized within her. She looked at the attractive women he would look at. . . . She had become him. She longed for these women. . . . And in this new empathy, in this pants role, as if in an opera, she thought she understood what it was to make love to another woman, to open the hidden underside of her, a secret food, to thrust yourself up in her, to feel her arching and thrashing like a puppet, to watch her later when she got up and walked around without you."[14]

In the everyday emotional intimacy of the couple, another kind of exchange may be effected. I think some of the strains in heterosexual relationships come through frustration of this attempt. When the woman's desire for merger is warded off by the man, her desire for what may be an especially female kind of intimacy is thwarted. She may seek this intimacy elsewhere, in a friend for example, but she wishes she had access to it with her mate as well. She wants the man to play with her in this way, being her (girl)friend as well as lover.

In a similar way the man may be frustrated in his desire for a kind of male-bonding within the marriage, for a wife who would share his interests, but even more importantly, his outward focus as an orientation to experience. He may become frustrated or exasperated with her concern for emotional connections. Heterosexual couples typically satisfy these needs through friendships outside the marriage, but a residual complaint against the partner remains, a feeling of not being understood and responded to. Within these desires and complaints, we can perceive the traces of the repressed homosexual interests of each.

The way unconscious homosexual interests can be played out in a heterosexual relationship is illustrated by a couple I know personally. Both the husband and wife have strong bonds with same-sex friends outside the marriage, and both often complain that these friendships are more satisfying in some ways than the marriage is. They try in vain to find in each other what they seem to find only in their friends. The husband is periodically jealous with regard to his wife. He thinks she pays attention to attractive men on the street or in restaurants, that she admires other men's bodies, and that she has a roving eye. The wife responds that she has only a passing interest in noticing attractive men, she has been faithful for years, and she is annoyed when this issue continues to surface. The husband can admit that he trusts her. He knows somehow that she has no real interest in other men, but still he is plagued by thoughts that she might. One can understand his jealousy as a consequence of his own interest in other men, projected onto his wife's more superficial interest. What this couple is unable to know about themselves is what causes trouble between them.

Just as lesbian couples have an interest in playing out unexplored parts of themselves, parts left behind in the identification and socialization process that determines gender roles, heterosexuals also come up against the lost parts of the self in their relationships. The exchanges of gender roles that gay couples employ may strike greater resistence in heterosexuals. Because their relationship is founded on opposition of gender, on masculinity and femininity as essence not as artifact, tampering with these categories may fundamentally threaten the bond between them.

To lesbians or gay men, the gender roles in heterosexual marriage appear contrived and rigid. The extent to which women and men are permitted to develop themselves within the confines of heterosexual bonding seems limited and oppressive. Even in relationships where both partners are well-meaning and committed to equality, the struggle to effect it seems more arduous than in gay relationships and ultimately seems to hit unalterable limits. Lesbians (or gay men) are not free from the constraints of gender, but the limits of their potential development are much wider.

Although gender roles in the culture at large are undergoing tremendous revision, there is also an undeniable back current that seeks to wash away these changes. Even where economics dictate the permanence of such changes as the necessity for women to work and children to go to day care, women's work remains devalued, day care lacks social commitment in terms of resources, and women are still expected to fulfill most of the traditional feminine roles in addition to their new responsibilities. This impossible requirement arises not simply from male insensitivity or female acquiescence, but from the deep fears of both men and women about how the institution of heterosexuality (or marriage based upon heterosexuality) will continue in the face of these changes. Likewise, the powerful social resistence to institutionalizing homosexual marriage expresses cultural doubts about the capability of heterosexual marriage to endure if it does not retain special status.

What takes place in heterosexual relationships in the way of gendered exchanges is thus often vicariously and unconsciously experienced. Women do identify with men and through identification see what is possible to do and become. Men may also have a deep sense of identification with women in intimate relationships and know more of the human potential for development through the relationship. They each find what is lost to the self in the other, and like the psychosexual exchange between primary and bisexual orientation in lesbian couples, they live this unlived part of the self through projective identification with the other.

The Ultimate Reversal

In an altogether different variation on these themes, Christine Downing writes of the kind of exchanges that took place for her, a lesbian, in a relationship with a gay man. She understands her love affairs with gay men on several levels. First, these relationships were part of a journey from her heterosexual past to her lesbian future. "It was as though I first needed to free myself from an inner heterosexism, from the fantasy of contrasexuality, from a focus on *otherness.*" Her friendships with gay men began as a bond based on "our shared longing to be free, internally as well as externally, of oppression by the prevailing conventions about masculinity and femininity."[15] Downing fell in love and had highly meaningful affairs with two gay men. About one of these she writes:

> I responded to him as though *he* were *my* anima [in Junigan terms, the female aspect of the psyche]—and only thus discovered how long I had coveted a relationship in which another would figure as anima for me, instead of my carrying that for him. He was my connection to soul, to the imaginal, to the intuitive and poetic, the dark and hidden, in myself. . . .
>
> I found that his femininity brought me more in touch with my own—whereas I had feared that loving someone "feminine" (male or female) would make me more "masculine." Our ways of being together gave me a new sense of the polymorphous possibilities of any relationship; for there were times when I was also anima or muse to him, Lou Salome to his Rilke.

Downing describes quite beautifully the couple's intimacy, which crossed all established lines between sexual and gender connections. In a way that probably surpasses the potential of other more traditional relationships (and here, traditional would have to include, ironically, relationships between gay men and between lesbians), she was able to encounter all the possibilities of gender exchange. Together they could experience both homosexuality and heterosexuality simultaneously. This account of love's possibilities forces us to question the familiar categories once again.

It seems that we can partake of lost bisexuality and bi-gender potentiality in whatever relationships we form. In each variation on human relating is the search for possibilities to pursue some kind of completion and wholeness. That this search is manifested in so many different forms of intimacy suggests how compelling its nature is for the human psyche. This analysis of the desire for a particular kind of other that allows people to find the unexpressed and undeveloped parts of themselves is an effort to reach beyond heterocentric thinking toward a more universal paradigm of attraction and bonding between partners of either sex.

Clinical
Meanings
and Further
Directions

12 | The question that always arises is what difference theories make in our lives. Theory is interesting for discussion and speculation, but it needs to be put to use somewhere as well. My hope is that this book will make some contribution to speculative thinking as well as meaningful application.

Speculation, if it is valuable, leads to further speculation, raises new questions, and points out future directions. Theories are useful at this level even when they are off-track; they stimulate others' thought. We are only beginning to think about human relationships, especially homosexual ones, in ways that reveal the complex interaction of culture with inherent potential.

Clinical Significance of Complementarity

The theory of complementarity is founded upon the idea that projections and introjections serve as powerful bonds in intimate relationships. These bonds are not simply defensive, as they are often regarded in the literature, but are also transformative. A corollary of this theory is that individuals seek out relationships to continue their own development, and relationships often are able to provide a medium for such development. Attractions between people reveal developmental motivations like those that bring people to therapy. In other words, relationships are akin to therapy in their power to transform. Even failed love has the capacity to do this. As Ethel Person notes, "When the outcome of love is unhappy, the lover may nonetheless have experienced the liberating effects of love and be able to preserve the fruits of that liberation, whether in expanded creativity, enlarged insight, or a subtle internal reordering of personality." Further, the lover's effect on the self does not end with the relationship. Past lovers are internalized and "continue to play a role in our emotional lives and self concepts."[1]

The parallel between intimate relationships and therapy has already been suggested in chapters 4 and 5 through the common ground of transference-countertransference dynamics and private intimacy. Employing this parallel in the other direction, we can understand how some salient issues between partners in lesbian relationships may come into the therapy relationship as well. Opportunities exist for the client (and for the therapist) to explore vicariously the varieties of sexual orientation, social sense of self (e.g., as deviant), and gender-related dimensions of personality. Here projections and introjections may be more heavily laden with fantasy than reality because little of the therapist's experience will be revealed. Nevertheless, the same mutual participation in each other's psychological formations takes place even while the overt work of therapy, perhaps quite different in nature, occurs.

Using the analysis of this thesis, a therapist may be able to appreciate the client's need for exploring the other side of lesbian experience, whichever it may be. Where a therapist is known or thought to be (or once to have been) heterosexual, for example, a primary lesbian client may unconsciously invite and participate in exchanges of a similar nature with her. However, the therapist may incorrectly assume that the client is struggling to change her sexual orientation, failing to appreciate instead her need for a new integration of this part of her psychic world without necessarily changing her object choice. In a similar way heterosexual clients in analytic therapy often discover homosexual aspects of themselves that do not get translated into change of object choice. Likewise, when the therapist is known or thought to be a lesbian, a client uses her as an object of her projections to explore "other" lesbian experience.

Because lesbian relationships have been seen as an unhealthy flight from healthy heterosexuality, the existing clinical literature on lesbian couples offers only a limited exploration of their dynamics. An atmosphere of mutual distrust has prevailed between traditional clinicians and lesbians who want help with their lives and relationships. In the past, lesbian couples did not commonly seek "marriage counseling." Social changes since the 1970s, however, have paved the way for a new understanding of homosexuality that allows for more helpful attitudes on the part of clinicians, attitudes not based on assumptions of pathology. In 1973 the American Psychiatric Association eliminated homosexuality as a diagnosis. Although this did not automatically transform prejudices in the professional community, it did pave the way for approaches that could bridge the two communities.[2] It is no longer uncommon for lesbians to seek couple therapy.

Freud's own granddaughter, Sophie Freud Lowenstein, herself a clinical social worker, wrote one of the first papers exploring a broad range of dimensions of lesbians' lives and advocating that therapists examine their own values about homosexuality. "To work with lesbians, therapists must have freed themselves of the conviction that a homosexual orientation is pathological, regressive, or immature. . . . It is just as important however, once this basic awareness has been secured, that lesbian clients be viewed as any other human being with a particular character structure who encounters problems in coping with life."[3] This means, of course, that we must develop a deeper understanding of both the pleasures and the pains of lesbians' lives and relationships.

Psychotherapy practice needs to be grounded in an awareness of the complicated interplay of social, cultural, and psychological determinants of individuals' lives. It is not enough to view human development strictly in intrapsychic terms if we are to have a fully informed grasp of clinical issues. The partnership of a primary lesbian and one who is bisexual highlights these differences. Although partners in other lesbian relationships may not have such different sexual histories and identification, more subtle variations sometimes approximate the more obvious ones. The terms of complementarity in more distinctly different couples may apply in a diffused version to other, less different couples. More research about lesbian couples would be useful to determine whether and how such differences affect relational dynamics.

Because these individual differences carry great meaning on both social and intrapsychic levels, they do not simply attract or serve as a bond. They also contain the seeds of conflict and tension. Like all differences between couples, they may threaten to disrupt the bond and attraction may fade. It is a commonplace in clinical work that individuals come to distrust and resent their partners for those differences that first drew them to each other. Understanding the source of the threat inherent in differences is often necessary for working through such difficulties. Envy of a partner's more socially valued attributes (or orientation) can be especially destructive if it is not explored and contained.

When the threat is more unconscious, it is especially important for a clinician to understand the dynamics involved. The psychological development possible in projective exchanges explored here is periodically unsettling. A lesbian couple whose relationship involves such complementarity is commonly not attuned to its full significance. Exploring differences in sexual orientation may be desirable in clinical work but may also stir resistance. The clinician can easily avoid complementarity, especially where she or he is relatively oblivious to its import and complexity.

A woman's painful sense of self as deviant may be heavily defended. Her defenses may be misinterpreted by her partner or therapist. Likewise, a woman's discomfort with moving into lesbian culture from the world of heterosexuality may be unacknowledged for long periods, even to herself. Both partners can resist confronting this as a problem. Such defenses limit the couple's intimacy and counteract the potential of the relationship for psychological exchange. Exploring these issues allows both women to bring a fuller sense of themselves to the relationship.

Differences in gendered sense of self are also weighted with meaning at various levels for therapists as well as clients. A sensitive therapist needs to be aware of her or his internal responses to nontraditional gender behavior, roles, and identity. Traditional therapists have commonly confounded their own defenses or biases with theory about "appropriate" identity.

Because lesbian (and gay male) development has until recently not received the thoughtful, unprejudiced attention that would provide a helpful clinical framework, a therapist perhaps may draw upon personal defenses and biases more unconsciously than in other clinical work. Although there is still much to understand about heterosexuality, the fear of homosexuality has encouraged ignorance of its potential for growth—which sometimes parallels that of heterosexuality and sometimes diverges from it greatly.

Social prejudice creates enormous individual suffering that has often been discounted in assessments of clients' issues. Paradoxically, this prejudice sometimes produces unusual psychological strengths, which are also not recognized as the remarkable achievements they are. The creative potential of lesbian relationships for ameliorating such suffering and drawing upon the strengths exists along with the more usual psychological possibilities inherent in all relationships. The necessity of keeping in mind both intrapsychic and interpersonal dimensions of experience, especially in work with minority groups, is underscored by a theory that draws upon both perspectives.

When couples are interviewed outside the clinical setting, with ample room to question and discuss, one discovers that the individuals themselves work out a story that explains the relationship to their satisfaction and makes their problems meaningful. This story carries themes that are psychologically significant to the couple, both individually and relationally. It provides a continuity to their history in spite of shifts and disruptions and helps them survive times of crisis. Generally, the story revolves around some kind of complementarity that they perceive between them. During my interviews, we together brought the stories to awareness when they had not already been conscious.

Over the course of my discussions, I observed how these stories worked best for both the couples and the individuals when thinking about their relationships. To provide a foundation of substance for a relationship, the story needs to be consensual and flexible, sometimes even contradictory. It needs a thread of continuity, however, through time and changing versions. Most important, the story needs to explain how each person makes use of the other, in the highest sense. It informs the couple about how to handle their differences, how to appreciate and profit from them.

Profiting from mutual story-building is often difficult in troubled relationships where differences pose some threat. The threat remains irreconcilable with the continued existence of the relationship until the partners begin to assign positive meaning to their differences, thereby allowing the differences to exist as a challenge and a bond that impels them to continue seeking each other out.

Understanding the nature and value of some of these stories is one aim of this book. Prior conceptions of how relationships work or are supposed to work provide a kind of map but inevitably hinder a genuine or spontaneous grasp of actual experience. Traditional ideas about lesbian relationships obscure the view, yet I also recognize that what I am creating here can be another hindrance. Thinking about this problem led me to value the process of story-building between couples more than the content of it. When therapy helps a couple to consolidate their own story until it defines their experience, it has probably achieved its major contribution.

Directions for Future Research

In this and previous chapters, the inadequacy of our understanding of lesbian development and relationships has been noted by suggesting areas in need of more attention. As the social climate becomes more favorable toward homosexuality, the opportunity exists for work not possible before. Prejudice has invaded empirical studies of homosexuality as much as it has theoretical ones.[4] Further, as lesbians and gay men are more willing to be identified, greater opportunities exist to discover the diversity of experience that characterizes homosexuality. Until (if ever) homosexuality has an entirely accepted place within the culture, however, we will deal with complications of social repression that distort whatever clinical and research investigations are undertaken.

Lesbian and gay relationships seem to be in a period of flux. Many lesbian couples are choosing to have children or to adopt them. The toll of AIDS on the gay male community in particular has altered relational patterns enormously, shifting communal values away from casual sex toward monogamous relationships. As Betty Berzon observes, "It appears that the age of the couple has come to the gay and lesbian community."[5]

At the same time, heterosexual culture seems also to be moving toward a renewed emphasis on stability and longevity of relationships in reaction to rising divorce rates and disruption of families. The 1980s and 1990s are coming to be known as a period in which the theme of family is paramount, both politically and socially. Lesbians and gay men are influenced by such a social trend and contribute to expanded notions of what constitutes a family.

It has often been argued that homosexual relationships do not endure as long as heterosexual ones largely because of their inherent pathology. Clearly, however, social forces and institutions have acted against homosexual couples in ways sufficient to undermine any kind of relationship.[6] Nevertheless, very little is really known about the developmental course and longevity of gay relationships. Research perhaps will offer greater understanding of when and how lesbian relationships are most likely to be successful, fulfilling, and enduring. The question of complementarity is intrinsic to such a pursuit. The mutuality necessary for a relationship to be a positive experience can probably never be fully defined; idiosyncratic needs and interests will always defy categorization. Nevertheless, a broad picture may emerge that at least suggests which factors support happiness and growth in coupling and which mediate against it, whether or not the relationship endures. Little data in the literature confirm or deny the role of differences in sexual orientation as an important dimension in lesbian relationships, only the intriguing evidence that many such relationships exist. Empirical research investigating the phenomenon of differences in orientation could provide valuable explorations or extensions.

A study investigating longevity in lesbian relationships would augment the present study by comparing relationships with and without differences in sexual history and identity. Does the complementarity engendered by such differences contribute to a relationship's endurance?

Another route would be to study the role of sequential relationships. Can patterns or shifts in the kinds of partners women choose from one relationship to the next be identified? The occurrence of repeating patterns or obvious shifts would be helpful in formulating ideas about this difference. Are they a developmental phenomenon, holding less psychological interest over time? Or do they represent an enduring source of complementarity?

A further question of research interest is whether fundamental differences in sexual orientation interact with the tendency toward merger often seen in lesbian relationships. Perhaps such differences are both desirable and threatening enough to give added thrust to the pull toward fusion—in an effort to embody or obliterate the other's difference. On the other hand, these differences may provide a firm distinction between self and other that allows the partners' engagement in merger as a transitory experience with a solid basis for differentiation afterward. They may counteract such a pull so the desired union can be more securely indulged without a more problematic confusion of self and other.

Research in other areas would contribute to an understanding of the dynamics of lesbian relationships, for example, the issue of parenting. Many lesbian couples are having children together, a phenomenon that the heterosexual world finds astonishing because it breaks all the rules about parenting and homosexual interests. It also poses dilemmas that heterosexual partners never face.

Observations and research presented by psychoanalysts Martha Kirkpatrick and Joyce McDougall indicate that both primary and bisexual lesbians desire to have children.[7] In the interviews I conducted, both primary and bisexual lesbians were also interested in bearing (not simply raising) children. More explorations of the correspondence between primary lesbian orientation and bisexual lesbian orientation and the desire for children might further delineate the relationship between gender identity and object choice, if only to show how complex and unpredictable it is. Thus do stereotypes crumble.

These data raise the intriguing question of how women in lesbian relationships decide who will bear children. In my own clinical and social experience, I have found that sometimes both women in a couple do become birth mothers (the term refers to the biological parent), and sometimes only one does. Sometimes the biological father is an unknown sperm donor, and sometimes he is a family friend. Thus sometimes two children in the same lesbian family have different mothers and different fathers; sometimes they have the same donor but different mothers; and sometimes they have the same mother but different donors. The complexity of these options confound those outside the family (and sometimes those inside). The gender roles and identities of the partners, of affiliated male co-parents, "uncles," or friends, and of the children are surely affected by these decisions and events.

Further questions arise. Does having children address the wounds that have been culturally inflicted upon lesbians? Does having children together affect lesbian couples' interactions in ways similar to or different from heterosexual couples? Because roles are usually not defined for lesbian couples, especially in parenting, children can be a source of both greater stress and greater bonding.

It would also be useful to gain a better understanding of other factors that contribute to the endurance of lesbian relationships. Do differences in attitudes of the families of origin contribute to the longevity of lesbian relationships? Do the "extended families" of lovers, close friends and former lovers survive over the years? How do the boundaries of the primary relationship shift or consolidate through time and in relation to the extended family, both lesbian and family of origin? How do lesbian communities change as society's tolerance of homosexuality changes, and how do these community changes affect individuals and couples?

This book began by providing perspective on the difficulty of using traditional theory that relies upon heterosexually oriented thinking in conceiving of complementary dimensions of lesbian relationships. Some fundamental reconception of this thinking is required to allow transcendence, as far as possible, of strongly maintained and culturally embedded notions that complementarity is inherently a matter of gender differences and disturbances. No doubt the present ideas move beyond conventional thinking only to a degree and also reflect culturally limited thinking. As many have acknowledged, human sexuality, and theories about it, is always a manifestation of the culture in which it is expressed.

We can see this influence most readily by analyzing the distortions that heterosexual prejudice brings to efforts at understanding homosexuality. What is more difficult to see are the underlying dynamics of heterosexuality, which is treated as a given, a natural expression that requires no analysis. As conventional thinking about homosexuality broadens, the unasked questions about heterosexuality will be raised more freely. Ultimately, a multifaceted approach for understanding all sexuality in a fuller, more complex way may result.

Appendix A:
The Interviews

Twelve interviews were conducted for this book: four with women who considered themselves to be primary lesbians, four with women who considered themselves to be bisexual lesbians, and four with couples that included one of each. I first chose women randomly from a network of social and professional acquaintances, then specifically selected women who identified one way or the other to complete the group. Each woman filled out forms 1 and 2, which determine their category and provide demographic data.

The individual interviews lasted from an hour to an hour and a half. The couple interviews lasted from an hour and a half to two hours. For both, I used the questions included herein. In every case we covered all of the given questions and also veered away from them at times to touch upon other matters that concerned the women or interested me. I wanted the interviews to be as spontaneous as possible under the circumstances, and they sometimes developed into discussions of lesbian development and relationships. Some of the discussions were fascinating in their own right.

In every case I was impressed by the perceptiveness of the women about issues in their lives and relationships. All live in the San Francisco Bay Area, which has well-established and diverse gay and lesbian communities. These communities, like the Bay Area as a whole, are sometimes regarded as being the political vanguard or, alternately, as being on the radical fringe. Like many members of these communities, the women I interviewed are well educated, sophisticated about political meanings of social norms, and relatively financially secure. These geographical and social distinctions mean that the subjects are not necessarily representative of lesbians elsewhere, or even of other lesbians in the Bay Area.

The women in the group were all middle class and worked in health-care professions (as administrators, consultants, nurses, psychotherapists, physical therapists, and researchers), in publishing (editing and writing), or in the sciences. They lack diversity not only in current class position (although the backgrounds of their families of origin ranged from working class to upper middle class), but also in racial background. One woman in the group identified herself as Hispanic, five identified as Jewish, and the rest as Caucasian.

Given the nature of this study, I wanted to involve women who were in their middle years, who had come to know themselves well and had settled into relationships that they hoped and expected would endure as lasting partnerships. Their ages varied from 36 to 52, with an average age of 40.2. All were currently involved in long-term relationships. The length of these relationships varied from 3 to 12 years, with an average of 7.3 years. When I finished writing the book, almost two years after the last interview, all of the couples were still together, and all but one of the individual women were still with the same partner. The commitment to themselves and each other that I had felt during the interviews was manifest in the endurance of the relationships.

Form 1

Please read over the following descriptions and check the one that best describes you. Probably no one will feel that a description exactly suits her, but if you feel one description does express your sense of yourself fairly well then check that one.

_____ A. In adolescence or my early 20s, I wondered about being gay. Whether I knew what it meant or not, I noticed that I was more interested in girls than boys. I didn't have significant sexual and romantic relationships with boys/men. If I got involved with men, it was primarily to find out if I was interested or else to cover lesbian interests I was uncomfortable with. In other words, I never really had a very strong or clear identity as a heterosexual. I probably thought that I was gay fairly early in my life.

_____ B. While I may have sometimes wondered if I was interested in girls/women at an early age, I was also quite interested in men as sexual and romantic partners. I had one or more significant relationships with a man. In other words, I did think of myself as heterosexual.

However, I realized at some point that I had a strong interest in women and began to question my identity. Eventually I got involved with a woman. Even though I may have some bisexual feelings, I think of myself as lesbian now.

_____ C. Neither of the above descriptions fits well enough for me to identify with it. This is how I would identify myself (use the back of this sheet if necessary):

_____

_____

_____

_____

_____

_____

_____

Form 2

Demographic Information

1. Name _____

2. Age _____ 3. Race/ethnic identity _____

4. Occupation _____

5. Highest educational level reached or in progress

_____

6. Ages of any children _____

7. My partner and I have been in a relationship for _____ years.

8. After reading the descriptions of lesbian identity on the preceding page I identified myself as (A, B, or C): _____, and I would identify my partner as (A, B, or C): _____.

Questions for Individual Interviews

1. How did you come to identify as lesbian?
   [age, experiences around coming out, relationships with men, sense of being different, etc.]

2. You identified yourself as _____ (A or B) on Form I. What are your thoughts about women who identify as (opposite)? [Do you have any ideas, feelings, or fantasies about women who are different from you in this way?]

3. Would you describe your current or former partners as _____ (A or B)? What are your thoughts about this?

4. If you see a pattern of similarity or difference in sexual identity with your partner(s), what effect, if any, do you think this has had on the relationship?

5. How do you think about or identify with the terms "butch" and "femme"?

6. How did you experience your family ties and alignments? Who in your family did you identify with or feel close to?

7. One idea behind this study is that differences in your personal histories of becoming a lesbian play some role in your attraction to each other. What are your thoughts about this?

Questions for Joint Interviews

To each woman:

1. How did you come to identify as lesbian?
   (age, experiences around coming out, relationships with men, sense of being different, etc.)

2. You identified yourself as _____ (A or B) on the questionnaire. Do you tend to get involved with women who are also _____ (A or B) or the opposite? What are your thoughts, feelings, fantasies about women who are in this group?

3. How did you experience your family ties and alignments? Who in your family did you identify with or feel close to?

To the couple:

4. Please tell me first what you'd like me to know about your relationship.

5. How do you think about or use the terms "butch" and "femme"?

6. How do differences in who you each are offer advantages and/or disadvantages in your relationship?

7. One idea behind this study is that differences in your personal histories of becoming a lesbian play some role in your attraction to each other. What are your thoughts about this?

Appendix B:
Survey of Therapists

Dear _____,

I am studying complementarity in lesbian relationships. That is, I am trying to develop an analysis of what attracts and bonds lesbians to each other aside from the traditional analysis of role-playing, butch-femme, etc. I am particularly interested in relationships between women where one partner is what has been called a "primary" lesbian—a woman who has been primarily with women rather than men—and lesbians who came out later after some serious involvement with a man or men. These are not absolutely discrete categories of course, but rather the two ends of a continuum. I am looking at women who would be toward opposite ends of this continuum who pair up with each other.

There is almost nothing in the literature on this type of lesbian couple. No studies have examined this variable, so I can't find any data to support the proposition that this type of connection may not be uncommon. Because the study is a theoretical one, I don't need rigorous empirical data, but an informal sampling would help.

What I'm asking of you is that you think about the couples you have seen in your clinical practice in the past two years and try to identify how many were couples of this kind. I'd also be interested in your own impressions of whether this was a significant dimension in their relationship, i.e., whether it appeared to be a meaningful variable for the couple.

Questionnaire

Think of lesbian orientation as a continuum, with one end representing a primary lesbian orientation, i.e., women who had little or no significant interest or involvement with men, and at the other end, women who did have significant involvement with men and came out as lesbian later.

Consider couples you have seen in your clinical practice over the last two years where both partners were older than 26:

1. In how many couples would the two women involved be found somewhere toward opposite ends of this continuum? _____

2. In how many couples would both women be found somewhere toward the same end of this continuum? _____

3. How many couples about whom you do not have any information on this dimension? _____

Thinking of couples in the first group, do you have a sense of whether this difference represented a meaningful distinction?

Notes

Chapter 1 | Thinking about Love and Lovers

1. Stephen Morin, "Heterosexual Bias in Psychological Research on Lesbianism and Male Homosexuality," *American Psychologist* 32 (1977): 629–37. Morin's survey of recent research on homosexuality reviews biases in research questions, methodology, subjects (e.g., neglect of lesbian subjects), and interpretation.

2. This fallacy is pointed out in M. E. Kite and K. Deaux, "Gender Belief Systems: Homosexuality and the Implicit Inversion Theory," *Psychology of Women Quarterly* 11 (1987): 83–96, and Natalie Eldridge and Lucia Gilbert, "Correlates of Relationship Satisfaction in Lesbian Couples," *Psychology of Women Quarterly* 14(1990): 43–62.

3. Sigmund Freud, "The Interpretation of Dreams," and "Three Contributions to the Theory of Sex," in *The Basic Writings of Sigmund Freud*, trans. A. A. Brill (New York: Modern Library, 1938).

4. Cultures that are matrilineally structured sometimes have less concern for establishing the biological father's rights and consequently are less concerned with life-long marriages. See Paula Gunn Allen, *The Sacred Hoop* (Boston: Beacon Press, 1986), and Will Roscoe, *The Zuni Man-woman* (Albuquerque: University of New Mexico Press, 1991) on Native American tribal cultures' traditions of serial monogamy.

5. Dorothy Dinnerstein, *The Mermaid and the Minotaur: Sexual Arrangements and Human Malaise* (New York: Harper and Row: 1976), argues that men impose monogamy on women to guarantee paternity. Philip Blumstein and Pepper Schwartz, *American Couples* (New York: William Morrow, 1983), note the disparity between lesbians and gay men in rates of monogamy.

6. In past centuries, high mortality rates for young and middle-aged adults often meant that men and women had more than one marriage if they lived

past the age of average life expectancy. What nature once determined, divorce now permits.

7. James Baldwin, *The Fire Next Time* (New York: Dial Press, 1963).

8. I argue this point elsewhere in "Psychotherapy and the Dynamics of Merger in Lesbian Relationships," in *Psychotherapy with Gay Men and Lesbians*, ed. Carol Cohen and Terry Stein (New York: Plenum, 1986), and "Barriers to Intimacy: Conflicts over Power, Dependency, and Nurturing in Lesbian Relationships," in *Lesbian Psychologies: Explorations and Challenges*, ed. Boston Lesbian Psychologies Collective (Urbana: University of Illinois Press, 1987).

9. For example, a number of papers on merger in lesbian relationships (including my own) emphasize it as a particularly lesbian problem. See Beverly Burch, "Psychological Merger in Lesbian Couples," *Family Therapy* 9 (1982): 201–7; Burch, "Another Perspective on Merger in Lesbian Relationships," in *A Handbook of Feminist Therapy: Women's Issues in Psychotherapy*, ed. Lynn Bravo Rosewater and Lenore Walker (New York: Springer, 1986); and Burch, "Dynamics of Merger"; Diane Elise, "Lesbian Couples: The Implications of Sex Differences in Separation-individuation," *Psychotherapy* 23 (1986): 305–10; Jo-Ann Krestan and Claudia Bepko, "The Problem of Fusion in the Lesbian Couple," *Family Process* 19, no. 3 (1980): 277–89. However, an earlier article describes the same problems in similar terms in heterosexual relationships. See Mark Karpel, "Individuation: From Fusion to Dialogue," *Family Process* 15 (1976): 65–82.

10. Frank Caprio, *Female Homosexuality: A Modern Study of Lesbianism* (New York: Grove Press, 1954) and Edmund Bergler, *Homosexuality: Disease or Way of Life?* (New York: Hill and Wang, 1957) were psychoanalysts who argued this position. Jonathan Katz, *Gay American History* (New York: Harper and Row, 1976) notes Bergler's and Caprio's influence on the psychoanalytic and medical community of their time.

11. Havelock Ellis, "Sexual Inversion," *Studies in the Psychology of Sex* (Philadelphia: F. A. Davis, 1928); Richard von Krafft-Ebing, *Psychopathia Sexualis* (New York: Stein and Day, 1965). Judy Grahn, *Another Mother Tongue* (Boston: Beacon Press, 1984), and Sasha Lewis, *Sunday's Women* (Boston: Beacon Press, 1979), discuss role-playing from a lesbian point of view. Esther Newton, "The Mythic Mannish Lesbian: Radclyffe Hall and the New Woman," *Signs: Journal of Women in Culture and Society* 9 (1984): 557–75, and Blumstein and Schwartz, *American Couples*, analyze role-playing in terms of the social forces of the 1920s and the 1950s.

12. Freud, "Three Contributions."

13. Ethel Spector Person, *Dreams of Love and Fateful Encounters: The Power of Romantic Passion* (New York: W. W. Norton, 1988).

14. Freud, "Three Contributions," 553–54.

15. B. Jowett, *The Works of Plato* (New York: Tudor, 1933), 317.

16. See Kenneth Lewes, *The Psychoanalytic Theory of Male Homosexuality* (New York: Simon and Schuster, 1988), and Christine Downing, *Myths*

and Mysteries of Same-Sex Love (New York: Crossroad Publishing, 1989), for two excellent discussions of Freud's views on homosexuality. Both find him to be highly inconsistent but nevertheless far more sympatic to the idea that homosexuality is simply a variation on normal human sexuality than most of his successors have been. Downing, as well as Peter Gay, *Freud: A Life for Our Time* (New York: W. W. Norton, 1988) note the homosexual strains in some of Freud's most important relationships with other men. Elaine Siegel, *Female Homosexuality: Choice without Volition* (Hillsdale, N.J.: The Analytic Press, 1988) refers to Charles W. Socarides's theory this way. Socarides's work, for example, *The Overt Homosexual* (New York: Grune and Stratton, 1968) is widely regarded as the preeminent psychoanalytic theory of homosexuality. Siegel's work is a recent extension of Socarides's.

17. Robert Stoller, *Observing the Erotic Imagination* (New Haven: Yale University Press, 1985); Joyce McDougall, "Identifications, Neoneeds, and Neosexualities," *International Journal of Psychoanalysis* 67 (1986): 19–31; and Abby Wolfson, "Toward the Further Understanding of Homosexual Women," *Journal of the American Psychoanalytic Association* 35 (1987): 165–73.

18. Most of the recent feminist analytic writings have affirmed this view in one way or another. See Nancy Chodorow, *The Reproduction of Mothering: Psychoanalysis and the Sociology of Gender* (Berkeley: University of California Press, 1978); Carol Gilligan, *In a Different Voice: Psychological Theory and Women's Development* (Cambridge: Harvard University Press, 1982); Jean Baker Miller, *Toward a New Psychology of Women* (Boston: Beacon Press, 1976), and Miller, "The Development of Women's Sense of Self," in *Works in Progress* (Wellesley: Stone Center for Developmental Services and Studies, 1984); Janet Surrey, "Self-in-Relation: A Theory of Women's Development," in *Works in Progress* (Wellesley: Stone Center for Developmental Services and Studies, 1985); and Emily Hancock, *The Girl Within* (New York: Fawcett Columbine, 1989).

19. Erik Erikson, *Childhood and Society* (New York: W. W. Norton, 1963).

20. Stoller, *Erotic Imagination*, 41.

21. Ibid., 101–2.

Chapter 2 | Other Love: Identities and Attractions

1. Ronald Bayer, *Homosexuality and American Psychiatry: The Politics of Diagnosis* (New York: Basic Books, 1981), and Vern Bullough, *Homosexuality: A History* (New York: New American Library, 1979), each provide perspective on this history.

2. Jeffrey Weeks, *Coming Out: Homosexual Politics in Britain, from the Nineteenth Century to the Present* (London: Quartet Press, 1977).

3. C. A. Tripp, *The Homosexual Matrix* (New York: McGraw-Hill, 1975); Evelyn Blackwood, "Sexuality and Gender in Certain Native American Tribes:

The Case of Cross-Gender Females," *Signs: Journal of Women in Culture and Society* 10 (1984): 27–42; Robert Stoller, *Observing the Erotic Imagination* (New Haven: Yale University Press, 1985).

4. Quoted in Martin Danneker, "Towards a Theory of Homosexuality," *Journal of Homosexuality* 9 (1984): 1

5. Alan Bell and Martin Weinberg, *Homosexualities: A Study of Diversity Among Men and Women* (New York: Simon and Schuster, 1978); Stoller, *Erotic Imagination;* Joyce McDougall, "Identifications, Neoneeds, and Neosexualities," *International Journal of Psychoanalysis* 67 (1986): 19–31; and Abby Wolfson, "Toward the Further Understanding of Homosexual Women," *Journal of the American Psychoanalytic Association* 35 (1987): 165–73.

6. Barbara Ponse, *Identities in the Lesbian World: The Social Construction of Self* (Westport: Greenwood Press, 1978), and Carla Golden, "Diversity and Variability in Women's Sexual Identities," in *Lesbian Psychologies: Explorations and Challenges*, ed. Boston Lesbian Psychologies Collective (Urbana: University of Illinois Press, 1987), use this term.

7. Golden, "Diversity and Variability," 25.

8. Ibid., 25–27.

9. This continuum resembles the one drawn in Alfred Kinsey et al., *Sexual Behavior in the Human Female* (Philadelphia: W. B. Saunders, 1953).

10. Vivienne Cass, "Homosexuality Identity: A Concept in Need of Definition," *Journal of Homosexuality* 9 (1984): 105–26.

11. Erik Erikson, *Childhood and Society* (New York: W. W. Norton, 1963).

12. Diane Richardson, "The Dilemma of Essentiality in Homosexual Theory," *Journal of Homosexuality* 9 (1984): 79–90.

13. Richardson, "The Dilemma of Essentiality," 86.

14. Sigmund Freud, "Three Contributions to the Theory of Sex," in *The Basic Writings of Sigmund Freud*, trans. A. A. Brill (New York: Modern Library, 1938).

15. Richard von Krafft-Ebing, *Psychopathia Sexualis* (New York: Stein and Day, 1965); Havelock Ellis, "Sexual Inversion," *Studies in the Psychology of Sex* (Philadelphia: F. A. Davis, 1928).

16. Bullough, *Homosexuality.*

17. K. Mannion, "Female Homosexuality: A Comprehensive Review of Theory and Research," *Dsad Catalogue of Selected Documents in Psychology* 2 (1976).

18. John Money, *Love and Love Sickness: The Science of Sex, Gender Difference, and Pair Bonding* (Baltimore: Johns Hopkins University Press, 1980), 32.

19. Richard Isay, *Being Homosexual* (New York: Farrar, Strauss, and Giroux, 1989), adopts the view that homosexuality is constitutionally determined, then uses psychoanalytic theory to formulate ideas about how experiences in the family shape the psychology of the homosexual child.

20. Sigmund Freud, "Female Sexuality," in *Collected Papers*, trans. Joan Riviere (London: Hogarth Press, 1953); 5:252–72.

21. Evelyn Hooker, "The Adjustment of the Male Overt Homosexual," *Journal of Projective Techniques* 21 (1957): 18–31; Virginia Armon, "Some Personality Variables in Overt Female Homosexuality," *Journal of Projective Techniques and Personality Assessment* 24 (1960): 293–309; Charles Weis and Robert Dain, "Ego Development and Sex Attitudes in Heterosexual and Homosexual Men and Women," *Archives of Sexual Behavior* 8 (1979): 341–56. See also Nanette Gartrell, "The Lesbian as a 'Single' Woman," *American Journal of Psychotherapy* 34 (1981): 502–10; and Robert Friedman, "The Psychoanalytic Model of Male Homosexuality: A Historical and Theoretical Critique," *Psychoanalytic Review* 73 (1986): 79–115.

22. Elaine Siegel, *Female Homosexuality: Choice without Volition* (Hillside, N.J.: The Analytic Press, 1988).

23. Sigmund Freud, "The Infantile Genital Organization of the Libido," in *Collected Papers*, 2: 244–49.

24. Nancy Chodorow, *The Reproduction of Mothering: Psychoanalysis and the Sociology of Gender* (Berkeley: University of California Press, 1978).

25. Stoller, *Erotic Imagination*: Margaret Nichols, "Lesbian Sexuality: Issues and Developing Theory," in *Lesbian Psychologies: Explorations and Challenges*, ed. Boston Lesbian Psychologies Collective (Urbana: University of Illinois Press, 1987).

26. Chodorow, *Reproduction of Mothering*, 128.

27. Ibid., 192–93.

28. In *Psychoanalyzing Psychoanalysis* (Baltimore: Johns Hopkins University Press, 1979), Marie Balmary deepens the psychoanalytic significance of Freud's identification with this myth, the full version of which expresses a generational transfer of "fault" from father to son to an extent greater than Freud acknowledged (or perhaps realized). She relates Freud's shift from an interpersonal perspective (the seduction theory) to an intrapsychic one (the fantasy theory) to Freud's turning away from knowledge of his own father's "fault."

29. See Max Herzberg, *Myths and Their Meaning* (Boston: Allyn and Bacon, 1962), and Edith Hamilton, *Mythology* (New York: Mentor, 1969) for two accounts of the story.

30. Stephen Mitchell, "Psychodynamics, Homosexuality, and the Question of Pathology," *Psychiatry* 41 (1978): 254–63 and "The Psychoanalytic Treatment of Homosexuality: Some Technical Considerations," *International Review of Psychoanalysis* 8 (1981): 63–80; Judd Marmor, *Homosexual Behavior: A Modern Reappraisal* (New York: Basic Books, 1980); Stanley Leavy, "Male Homosexuality Reconsidered," *International Journal of Psychoanalysis* 11 (1985): 155–74; Stoller, *Erotic Imagination*; Friedman, "The Psychoanalytic Model," 79–115; Wolfson, "Toward the Further Understanding," 165–73; Lewes, *Psychoanalytic Theory*; Isay, *Being Homosexual*.

31. Beverly Burch, "Heterosexuality, Bisexuality, and Lesbianism: Rethinking Psychoanalytic Views of Women's Sexual Object Choice," *Psychoanalytic Review* (in press).

32. Albert Bandura, *Principles of Behavior Modification* (New York: Holt, Rhinehart, and Winston, 1969); M. P. Feldman and M. J. MacCullough, *Homosexual Behavior: Therapy and Assessment* (Oxford: Pergamon Press, 1971).

33. Kinsey, *Sexual Behavior in the Human Female*, 451.

34. Hooker, "The Adjustment of the Male Overt Homosexual," 18–31; Armon, "Some Personality Variables," 293–309; Weis and Dain, "Ego Development and Sex Attitudes," 341–56; Gartrell, "The Lesbian as a 'Single' Woman," 502–10; and Friedman, "The Psychoanalytic Model of Male Homosexuality," 79–115.

35. K. Plummer, *Sexual Stigma: An Interactionist Account* (London: Routledge and Kegan Paul, 1975); Vivienne Cass, "Homosexual Identity Formation: A Theoretical Model," *Journal of Homosexuality* 4 (1979): 219–35; Richard Troiden, "Becoming Homosexual: A Model for Gay Identity," *Psychiatry* 42 (1979): 362–73; and Eli Coleman, "Developmental Stages of the Coming Out Process," *Journal of Homosexuality* 7 (1981–82): 31–43.

36. Erikson, *Childhood*, 261.

37. R. Sablonsky, *The Process of Acquiring a Lesbian Identity* (Berkeley: California School of Professional Psychology, 1981); Mary Lou Butler, "Coming Out in the Middle Years: Issues for Women," paper delivered at the annual meeting of the American Psychological Association, 1983.

38. Plummer, *Sexual Stigma*; Cass, "Homosexual Identity Formation"; Troiden, "Becoming Homosexual"; Coleman, "Developmental Stages."

39. Cass, "Homosexual Identity Formation," 220.

40. Julia Penelope Stanley and Susan Wolfe, *The Coming Out Stories* (Watertown: Persephone Press, 1980); Sablonsky, *Acquiring a Lesbian Identity*.

41. Stanley and Wolfe, *Coming Out Stories*, 57, 100.

42. Ponse, *Identities*, 131.

43. Ibid., 154.

44. Cass, "Homosexual Identity Formation."

45. Jeanne Miranda and Michael Storms, "Psychological Adjustment of Lesbians and Gay Men," *Journal of Counseling and Development* 68, no. 1 (1989): 41–45.

46. Charles W. Socarides, *The Overt Homosexual* (New York: Grune and Stratton, 1968); Charles W. Socarides, "Psychoanalytic Perspectives on Female Homosexuality," *American Journal of Psychotherapy* 34 (1981): 510–15; Joyce McDougall, *Plea for a Measure of Abnormality* (New York: International Universities Press, 1980). See also Beverly Burch, "Psychological Merger in Lesbian Couples," *Family Therapy* 9 (1982): 201–7; Burch, "Psychotherapy and the Dynamics of Merger in Lesbian Relationships," in *Psychotherapy with Gay Men and Lesbians*, ed. Carol Cohen and Terry Stein (New York: Plenum, 1986); and Diane Elise, "Lesbian Couples: The Implications of Sex Differences in Separation-individuation," *Psychotherapy* 23 (1986): 305–10.

Chapter 3 | The Road Not Taken

1. Stephen Morin, "Heterosexual Bias in Psychological Research on Lesbianism and Male Homosexuality," *American Psychologist* 32 (1977): 629–37.

2. Marcia Salner, "Validity in Human Science Research," *Saybrook Review* 6 (1986): 107–30.

3. Betty Berzon, *Permanent Partners* (New York: E. P. Dutton, 1988), 34.

4. Berzon, *Permanent Partners*, 29.

5. Philip Blumstein and Pepper Schwartz, *American Couples* (New York: William Morrow, 1983).

6. Donna Tanner, *The Lesbian Couple* (Lexington: D. C. Heath, 1978).

Chapter 4 | The Psychological Function of Relationships

1. Sigmund Freud, "Further Recommendations on the Technique of Psychoanalysis: Observations on Transference-love," in *Collected Papers*, trans. Joan Riviere (London: Hogarth Press, 1953), 2: 387.

2. Ethel Spector Person, *Dreams of Love and Fateful Encounters: The Power of Romantic Passion* (New York: W. W. Norton, 1988), 114–16.

3. Person, *Dreams of Love*, 122.

4. Sigmund Freud, "The Dynamics of Transference," in *Collected Papers*, 2:312–13.

5. W. R. D. Fairbairn, "A Revised Psychopathology of the Psychoses and Psychoneuroses," and "Object Relations and Dynamic Structure," in *Psychoanalytic Studies of the Personality* (London: Routledge and Kegan Paul, 1952); Thomas Ogden, *The Matrix of the Mind: Object Relations and the Psychoanalytic Dialogue* (Northvale: Jason Aronson, 1986).

6. Martin Bergmann, "On the Intrapsychic Function of Falling in Love," *Psychoanalytic Quarterly* 49 (1980): 60.

7. Bergmann, "Intrapsychic Function," 68, 74.

8. Bernard Murstein, *Who Will Marry Whom? Theories and Research in Marital Choice* (New York: Springer, 1976), 26.

9. Robert Knight, "Introjection, Projection, and Identification," *Psychoanalytic Quarterly* 9 (1940): 340.

10. Joyce McDougall, "Eve's Reflection: On the Homosexual Components of Female Sexuality," in *Between Analyst and Patient: New Dimensions in Countertransference and Transference*, ed. H. C. Meyers (New York: Analytic Press, 1986), 215.

11. John Money, *Love and Love Sickness: The Science of Sex, Gender Difference, and Pair Bonding* (Baltimore: Johns Hopkins University Press, 1980), 65.

12. Money, *Love and Love Sickness*, 67.

13. Ibid., 67–68.

14. Martin Stein, "The Marriage Bond," *Psychoanalytic Quarterly* 25 (1956): 238–59; Bergmann, "Intrapsychic Function". Person, *Dreams of Love*.

15. Nathaniel Ross, "Affect as Cognition: With Observations on the Mean-

ings of Mystical States," *International Review of Psychoanalysis* 2 (1975): 91.

16. Person, *Dreams of Love*, 122.

17. Fairbairn, "Object Relations."

18. Nancy Chodorow, *The Reproduction of Mothering: Psychoanalysis and the Sociology of Gender* (Berkeley: University of California Press, 1978); Carol Gilligan, *In a Different Voice: Psychological Theory and Women's Development* (Cambridge: Harvard University Press, 1982); Jean Baker Miller, *Toward a New Psychology of Women* (Boston: Beacon Press, 1976), and Miller, "The Development of Women's Sense of Self," in *Works in Progress* (Wellesley: Stone Center for Developmental Services and Studies, 1984); Janet Surrey, "Self-in-Relation: A Theory of Women's Development," in *Works in Progress* (Wellesley: Stone Center for Developmental Services and Studies, 1985); and Emily Hancock, *The Girl Within* (New York: Fawcett Columbine, 1989). See also Joan Berzoff, "Fusion and Heterosexual Women's Friendships: Implications for Expanding Our Adult Developmental Theories," *Women and Therapy* 8 (1989): 93–107; and Doris Silverman, "What Are Little Girls Made Of?" *Psychoanalytic Psychology* 4 (1987): 315.

19. Andre Green, *On Private Madness* (Madison: International Universities Press, 1986).

20. D. W. Winnicott, *Playing and Reality* (London: Tavistock Publications, 1971), 110.

21. Madeleine Davis and David Wallbridge, *Boundary and Space: An Introduction to the Work of D. W. Winnicott* (New York: Bruner-Mazel, 1981), 65.

22. D. W. Winnicott, "Transitional Objects and Transitional Phenomena," in *Playing and Reality*. In "The Transitional Oedipal Relationship in Female Development," *International Journal of Psychoanalysis* 68 (1987): 485–98, Thomas Ogden extends this concept to describe how the child takes in the existence of new objects (in this case the father) in his conception of female oedipal experience.

23. Green, *Private Madness*, 47.

24. Ibid., 47–48, emphasis added.

25. Ibid., 48.

Chapter 5 | Unconscious Conversations

1. Paula Heimann, "On Countertransference," *International Journal of Psychoanalysis* 31 (1950): 81–84.

2. Sigmund Freud, "Group Psychology and the Analysis of the Ego," in *Standard Edition* (London: Hogarth Press, 1921), 18: 21.

3. Helene Deutsch, *The Psychology of Women* (New York: Grune and Stratton, 1944); Robert Fliess, "The Metapsychology of the Analyst," *Psychoanalytic Quarterly* 11 (1942): 211–27; David Beres, and Jacob Arlow, "Fantasy and Identification in Empathy," *Psychoanalytic Quarterly* 43 (1974): 26–50;

Thomas Ogden, *The Matrix of the Mind: Object Relations and the Psychoanalytic Dialogue* (Northvale: Jason Aronson, 1986).

4. James Grotstein, *Splitting and Projective Identification* (New York: Jason Aronson, 1981). Cf. Melanie Klein, "Notes on Some Schizoid Mechanisms" and "Some Theoretical Conclusions Regarding the Emotional Life of the Infant," in *Envy and Gratitude and Other Works, 1946–1963* (New York: Free Press, 1975); W. R. Bion, *Second Thoughts* (New York: Jason Aronson, 1967); Roy Schafer, "Generative Empathy in the Treatment Situation," *Psychoanalytic Quarterly* 28 (1959): 342–73; Thomas Ogden, *Projective Identification and Psychotherapeutic Technique* (New York: Jason Aronson, 1982). Grotstein, for example, thinks of empathy as a sublimated form of projective identification.

5. Klein, "Schizoid Mechanisms"; Arthur Malin and James Grotstein, "Projective Identification in the Therapeutic Process," *International Journal of Psychoanalysis* 47 (1966): 26–31; Grotstein, *Splitting.*

6. Klein, "Theoretical Considerations," 68–69.

7. See Beverly Burch, "Melanie Klein's Work: An Adaptation in Practice," *Clinical Social Work Journal* 16 (Summer 1988): 125–42, and "Mourning and Failure to Mourn: An Object-Relations View," *Contemporary Psychoanalysis* 25 (Oct. 1989): 608–23 for a more detailed discussion of these processes in early development.

8. Anna Freud, *The Ego and the Mechanisms of Defence* (New York: International Universities Press, 1936), 133.

9. Malin and Grotstein, "Projective Identification," and Grotstein, *Splitting,* argue this position at length. In "Introjection, Projection, and Identification," *Psychoanalytic Quarterly* 9 (1940): 334–41, Robert Knight clarifies that identification is the outcome, while projection and introjection are the mechanisms.

10. Malin and Grotstein, "Projective Identification," 27.

11. Robert Langs, *The Therapeutic Interaction* (New York: Jason Aronson, 1976), and *The Bipersonal Field* (New York: Jason Aronson, 1976); Ogden, *Projective Identification.*

12. Martin Wangh, "The Evocation of a Proxy," *Psychoanalytic Study of the Child* 17 (1962): 453.

13. Michael Basch, "Empathic Understanding: A Review of the Concept and Some Theoretical Considerations," *Journal of the American Psychoanalytic Association* 31 (1983): 101–26; Robert Stolorow, Bernard Brandchaft, and George Atwood, *Psychoanalytic Treatment* (Hillsdale: Analytic Press, 1987). Self psychologists tend to differ from object-relations theorists in this respect.

14. Ogden, *Projective Identification,* 21.

15. Malin and Grotstein, "Projective Identification," 28.

16. Robert Langs, *Classics in Psychoanalytic Technique* (New York: Jason Aronson, 1981).

17. Jay Greenburg and Stephen Mitchell, *Object Relations in Psychoanalytic Theory* (Cambridge: Harvard University Press, 1983), and Stephen

Mitchell, *Relational Concepts in Psychoanalysis: An Integration* (Cambridge: Harvard University Press, 1988) are among many who offer valuable accounts of this trend.

18. Martin Stein, "The Marriage Bond," *Psychoanalytic Quarterly* 25 (1956): 238–59. He, too, notes how few psychoanalytic studies of marriage exist.

19. Sigmund Freud, "Certain Neurotic Mechanisms in Jealousy, Paranoia, and Homosexuality," in *Collected Papers*, trans. Joan Riviere (London: Hogarth Press, 1953), 2: 236.

20. Melanie Klein, "On Identification," in *Envy and Gratitude and Other Works*.

21. M. Eugenia Huneeus, "A Dynamic Approach to Marital Problems," *Social Casework* 44 (1963), 142.

22. Huneeus, "A Dynamic Approach," 143.

23. Barbara Gray Ellis, "Unconscious Collusion in Marital Interaction," *Social Casework* 45 (1964): 79.

24. Polly Crisp, "Projective Identification: Clarification in Relation to Object Choice," *Psychoanalytic Psychology* 5 (1988): 396.

25. Crisp, "Projective Identification," 396.

26. Ethel Spector Person, *Dreams of Love and Fateful Encounters: The Power of Romantic Passion* (New York: W. W. Norton, 1988).

Chapter 6 | Psychosexual Interests, Past, Present, and Future

1. Sigmund Freud, "Three Contributions to the Theory of Sex," in *The Basic Writings of Sigmund Freud*, trans. A. A. Brill (New York: Modern Library, 1938).

2. Kenneth Lewes, *The Psychoanalytic Theory of Male Homosexuality* (New York: Simon and Schuster, 1988), 17.

3. Joyce McDougall, "Eve's Reflection: On the Homosexual Components of Female Sexuality," in *Between Analyst and Patient: New Dimensions in Countertransference and Transference*, ed. H. C. Meyers (New York: Analytic Press, 1986), 215, 219–20.

4. This term is from Polly Crisp, "Projective Identification: Clarification in Relation to Object Choice," *Psychoanalytic Psychology* 5 (1988): 389–402.

5. Melanie Klein, "Some Theoretical Conclusions Regarding the Emotional Life of the Infant," in *Envy and Gratitude and Other Works, 1946–1963* (New York: Free Press, 1975), 68.

Chapter 7 | Deviant Selves and Different Selves

1. Vivienne Cass, "Homosexual Identity Formation: A Theoretical Model," *Journal of Homosexuality* 4 (1979): 219–35.

2. Nancy Chodorow, *The Reproduction of Mothering: Psychoanalysis and the Sociology of Gender* (Berkeley: University of California Press, 1978);

Ethel Spector Person, *Dreams of Love and Fateful Encounters: The Power of Romantic Passion* (New York: W. W. Norton, 1988).

3. Emily Hancock, *The Girl Within* (New York: Fawcett Columbine, 1989), 18–19.

4. Jo-Ann Krestan and Claudia Bepko, "The Problem of Fusion in the Lesbian Couple," *Family Process* 19, no. 3 (1980): 277–89; Beverly Burch, "Psychological Merger in Lesbian Couples," *Family Therapy* 9 (1982): 201–7; Burch "Another Perspective on Merger in Lesbian Relationships," in *A Handbook of Feminist Therapy: Women's Issues in Psychotherapy*, ed. Lynne Bravo Rosewater and Lenore Walker (New York: Springer, 1985); and Burch, "Psychotherapy and the Dynamics of Merger in Lesbian Relationships," in *Psychotherapy with Gay Men and Lesbians*, ed. Carol Cohen and Terry Stein (New York: Plenum, 1986); Susan Krieger, "Lesbian Identity and Community: Recent Social Science Literature," *Signs: Journal of Women in Culture and Society* 8 (1982): 91–108; Krieger, *The Mirror Dance: Identity in a Women's Community* (Philadelphia: Temple University Press, 1983); Phyllis Kaufman, Elizabeth Harrison, and Mary Lou Hyde, "Distancing for Intimacy in Lesbian Relationships," *American Journal of Psychiatry* 141 (1984): 530–33; Sallyann Roth, "Psychotherapy with Lesbian Couples: Individual Issues, Female Socialization, and the Social Context," *Journal of Marital and Family Therapy* 11 (1985): 273–86; Diane Elise, "Lesbian Couples: The Implications of Sex Differences in Separation-Individuation," *Psychotherapy* 23 (1986): 305–10; Joyce Lindenbaum, "The Shattering of an Illusion: The Problem of Competition in Lesbian Relationships," in *Competition: A Feminist Taboo?* ed. Valerie Miner and Helen Longino (New York: Feminist Press, 1987); Valory Mitchell, "Using Kohut's Self Psychology in Work with Lesbian Couples," *Women and Therapy* 8 (1988).

5. Person, *Dreams of Love*, 127–29.

6. Mark Karpel, "Individuation: From Fusion to Dialogue," *Family Process* 15 (1976): 65–82; Krestan and Bepko, "Problem of Fusion"; Burch, "Psychological Merger," "Another Perspective," and "Psychotherapy and Dynamics of Merger"; Kaufman, Harrison, and Hyde, "Distancing for Intimacy"; Roth, "Psychotherapy with Lesbian Couples"; Elise, "Lesbian Couples."

7. Chodorow, *The Reproduction of Mothering*; Carol Gilligan, *In a Different Voice: Psychological Theory and Women's Development* (Cambridge: Harvard University Press, 1982); Jean Baker Miller, *Toward a New Psychology of Women* (Boston: Beacon Press, 1976), and "The Development of Women's Sense of Self," in *Works in Progress* (Wellesley: Stone Center for Developmental Services and Studies, 1984); Janet Surrey, "Self-in-Relation: A Theory of Women's Development," in *Works in Progress* (Wellesley: Stone Center for Developmental Services and Studies, 1985); Doris Silverman, "What Are Little Girls Made Of?" *Psychoanalytic Psychology* 4 (1987): 315; Joan Berzoff, "Fusion and Heterosexual Women's Friendships: Implications for Expanding Our Adult Developmental Theories," *Women and Therapy* 8 (1989): 93–107; Hancock, *Girl Within*.

8. Julie Mencher, "Intimacy in Lesbian Relationships: A Critical Re-examination of Fusion," in *Works in Progress* (Wellesley: Stone Center for Developmental Services and Studies, 1990).

9. Carol Becker, *Unbroken Ties: Lesbian Ex-lovers* (Boston: Alyson Publications, 1988).

10. Burch, "Psychological Merger," "Another Perspective," and "Psychotherapy and Dynamics of Merger"; Elise, "Lesbian Couples"; Lindenbaum, "Shattering of an Illusion."

11. Mitchell, "Using Kohut's," 158, 164–65.

12. Mencher, "Intimacy in Lesbian Relationships."

13. Berzoff, "Fusion," 105–6.

14. Person, *Dreams of Love*, 137.

Chapter 8 | What Gender Signifies

1. Adria Schwartz, "Some Notes on the Development of Female Gender Role Identity," in *Psychoanalysis and Women: Contemporary Reappraisals*, ed. Judith Alpert (Hillsdale: The Analytic Press, 1986).

2. Phyllis Tyson, "A Developmental Line of Gender Identity, Gender Role, and Choice of Object Love," *Journal of the American Psychoanalytic Association* 30 (1982): 83–84.

3. Schwartz, "Female Gender Role Identity." She follows this tradition herself, although she does allow for other possibilities.

4. In fact, this disguised heterosexuality was at the heart even of Freud's argument for a primary bisexuality. See Christine Downing, *Myths and Mysteries of Same-Sex Love* (New York: Crossroad Publishing, 1989), and Judith Butler, "Gender Trouble, Feminist Theory, and Psychoanalytic Discourse," in *Feminism/Postmodernism*, ed. Linda Nicholson (New York: Routledge, 1990) for two different approaches to the same conclusion.

5. Schwartz, "Female Gender Role Identity," 58.

6. Irene Fast, "Aspects of Early Gender Development: Toward a Reformulation" *Psychoanalytic Psychology* 7 (1990): 105–17.

7. Sherry Ortner and Harriet Whitehead, *Sexual Meanings: The Cultural Construction of Gender and Sexuality* (Cambridge: Cambridge University Press, 1984).

8. Jane Flax, *Thinking Fragments* (Berkeley: University of California Press, 1990), 22.

9. Butler, "Gender Trouble," 328.

10. Ibid., 331, 338.

11. Evelyn Blackwood, "Sexuality and Gender in Certain Native American Tribes: The Case of Cross-gender Females," *Signs: Journal of Women in Culture and Society* 10 (1984): 27–42; Paula Gunn Allen, *The Sacred Hoop* (Boston: Beacon Press, 1986); Will Roscoe, *The Zuni Man-woman* (Albuquerque: University of New Mexico Press, 1991).

12. Elizabeth Wilson, "Forbidden Love," *Feminist Studies* 10 (1984): 213–26;

Ethel Spector Person, *Dreams of Love and Fateful Encounters: The Power of Romantic Passion* (New York: W. W. Norton, 1988).

13. Sue Vargo, "The Effects of Women's Socialization on Lesbian Couples," in *Lesbian Psychologies: Explorations and Challenges*, ed. Boston Lesbian Psychologies Collective (Urbana: University of Illinois Press, 1987), 163.

14. Vargo, "Effects of Women's Socialization," 163.

15. Joyce McDougall, "Eve's Reflection: On the Homosexual Components of Female Sexuality," in *Between Analyst and Patient: New Dimensions in Countertransference and Transference*, ed. H. C. Meyers (New York: Analytic Press, 1986).

16. Fast, "Aspects of Early Gender Development," 108.

17. Ibid., 110.

18. John Money and Anke Erhardt, *Man and Woman, Boy and Girl* (Baltimore: Johns Hopkins University Press, 1972).

19. Randall Jones and John DeCecco, "The Femininity and Masculinity of Partners in Heterosexual and Homosexual Relationships," *Journal of Homosexuality* 8 (1982): 37–44; Ronald LaTorre and Kristina Wendenburg, "Psychological Characteristics of Bisexual, Heterosexual, and Homosexual Women," *Homosexuality and Social Sex Roles* (New York: Haworth Press, 1983).

20. Sue Oldham, Doug Farnil, and Ian Ball, "Sex-role Identity of Female Homosexuals," *Journal of Homosexuality* 8 (1982): 41–46.

21. John Gagnon and William Simon, *Sexual Conduct: The Social Sources of Human Sexuality* (Chicago: Aldine Publishing, 1973); Karla Jay, and Allan Young, *The Gay Report: Lesbians and Gay Men Speak Out About Sexual Experiences and Lifestyles* (New York: Summit Books, 1977); Alan Bell and Martin Weinberg, *Homosexualities: A Study of Diversity Among Men and Women* (New York: Simon and Schuster, 1978); Sasha Lewis, *Sunday's Women: Lesbian Life Today* (Boston: Beacon Press, 1979); Philip Blumstein and Pepper Schwartz, *American Couples* (New York: William Morrow, 1983); Margaret Schneider, "The Relationships of Cohabiting Lesbian and Heterosexual Couples: A Comparison," *Psychology of Women Quarterly* 10 (1986): 234–39.

22. Jeanne Marecek, Stephen Finn, and Mona Cardell, "Gender Roles in the Relationships of Lesbians and Gay Men," *Journal of Homosexuality* 8 (1982): 45–50; Letitia Anne Peplau, Christine Padesky, and Mykol Hamilton, "Satisfaction in Lesbian Relationships," *Journal of Homosexuality* 8 (1982): 23–35; Mayta Caldwell and Letitia Anne Peplau, "The Balance of Power in Lesbian Relationships," *Sex Roles* 10 (1984): 587–99; Jean Lynch and Mary Ellen Reilly, "Role Relationships: Lesbian Perspectives," *Journal of Homosexuality* 12 (1985–86): 53–69.

23. Blumstein and Schwartz, *American Couples*; Lynch and Reilly, "Role Relationships."

24. Jonathan Katz, *Gay American History* (New York: Harper and Row, 1976), 7.

25. Wilson, "Forbidden Love," 215–16.

26. Esther Newton, "The Mythic Mannish Lesbian: Radclyffe Hall and the

New Woman," *Signs: Journal of Women in Culture and Society* 9 (1984): 557–75.

27. Wilson, "Forbidden Love," 216.

Chapter 9 | Gender Devices and Desires

1. Jeanne Marecek, Stephen Finn, and Mona Cardell, "Gender Roles in the Relationships of Lesbians and Gay Men," *Journal of Homosexuality* 8 (1982): 45–50.

2. John Gagnon and William Simon, *Sexual Conduct: The Social Sources of Human Sexuality* (Chicago: Aldine Publishing, 1973); Julia Penelope Stanley and Susan Wolfe, *The Coming Out Stories* (Watertown: Persephone Press, 1980); Judy Grahn, *Another Mother Tongue* (Boston: Beacon Press, 1984).

3. Amber Hollibaugh and Cherrie Moraga, "What We're Rolling Around in Bed With: Sexual Silences in Feminism," in *Powers of Desire: The Politics of Sexuality*, ed. Ann Snitow, Christine Stansell, and Sharon Thompson (New York: Monthly Review Press, 1983); Joan Nestle, "The Fem Question," in *Pleasure and Danger: Exploring Female Sexuality*, ed. Caole Vance (Boston: Routledge and Kegan Paul, 1984).

4. Judy Grahn, *Another Mother Tongue* (Boston: Beacon Press, 1984); Elizabeth Wilson, "Forbidden Love," *Feminist Studies* 10 (1984): 213–26.

5. Wilson, "Forbidden Love," 219.

6. Ibid., 224.

7. Ibid.

8. Kenneth Lewes, *The Psychoanalytic Theory of Male Homosexuality* (New York: Simon and Schuster, 1988).

9. See Christine Downing's [*Myths and Mysteries of Same-Sex Love* (New York: Crossroad Publishing, 1989)] discussion of same-sex love among the gods and goddesses.

10. Adrienne Rich, "Compulsory Heterosexuality and Lesbian Experience," *Signs: Journal of Women in Culture and Society* 5 (1980): 631–60; Janice Raymond, *A Passion for Friends: Toward a Philosophy of Female Affection* (Boston: Beacon Press, 1986).

11. Robert Knight, "Introjection, Projection, and Identification," *Psychoanalytic Quarterly* 9 (1940): 334–41; Bernard Murstein, *Who Will Marry Whom? Theories and Research in Marital Choice* (New York: Springer, 1976); Martin Bergmann, "On the Intrapsychic Function of Falling in Love," *Psychoanalytic Quarterly* 49 (1980): 56–77.

12. Bergmann, "Intrapsychic Function," 74.

Chapter 10 | Literary Illusions

1. Alfred Kinsey, Wardell Pomeroy, and Clyde Martin, *Sexual Behavior in the Human Male* (Philadelphia: W. B. Saunders, 1948); Alfred Kinsey et al., *Sexual Behavior in the Human Female* (Philadelphia: W. B. Saunders, 1953).

2. Havelock Ellis, "Sexual Inversion," *Studies in the Psychology of Sex* (Philadelphia: F. A. Davis, 1928), 222–23.

3. Lillian Faderman, *Surpassing the Love of Men: Romantic Friendship and Love between Women from the Renaissance to the Present* (New York: William Morrow, 1981).

4. Faderman, *Surpassing the Love.*

5. Jonathan Katz, *Gay American History* (New York: Harper and Row, 1976); Lillian Faderman, "The Morbidification of Love Between Women," *Journal of Homosexuality* 4 (1978): 73–90; Sheila Jeffreys, *The Spinster and her Enemies: Feminism and Sexuality 1880–1930* (London: Pandora Press, 1985).

6. Jeffreys, *Spinster.*

7. Esther Newton, "The Mythic Mannish Lesbian: Radclyffe Hall and the New Woman," *Signs: Journal of Women in Culture and Society* 9 (1984): 557–75.

8. Newton, "Mythic Mannish Lesbian," 573.

9. Frank Caprio, *Female Homosexuality: A Modern Study of Lesbianism* (New York: Grove Press, 1954); Edmund Bergler, *Homosexuality: Disease or Way of Life?* (New York: Hill and Wang, 1957); In *Gay American History,* Katz details the prevalence of this thinking throughout the professional establishment in modern times.

10. Sasha Lewis, *Sunday's Women: Lesbian Life Today* (Boston: Beacon Press, 1979); Judy Grahn, *Another Mother Tongue* (Boston: Beacon Press, 1984).

11. Philip Blumstein and Pepper Schwartz, *American Couples* (New York: William Morrow, 1983), 44.

12. Lovat Dickson, *Radclyffe Hall at the Well of Loneliness* (New York: Charles Scribner's Sons, 1975).

13. Dickson, *Radclyffe Hall.*

14. Radclyffe Hall, *The Well of Loneliness* (New York: Doubleday, 1974), Commentary.

15. Dickson, *Radclyffe Hall,* 25, 161.

16. Elizabeth Wilson, "Forbidden Love," *Feminist Studies* 10 (1984): 213.

17. Buffy Dunker, "Aging Lesbians: Observations and Speculations," in *Lesbian Psychologies: Explorations and Challenges,* ed. Boston Lesbian Psychologies Press (Urbana: University of Illinois Press, 1987), 74.

18. Julia Penelope Stanley and Susan Wolfe, *The Coming Out Stories* (Watertown: Persephone Press, 1980).

19. Newton, "Mythic Mannish Lesbian."

20. Dickson, *Radclyffe Hall,* 37.

21. Hall, *Well of Loneliness,* 430.

22. The series of lesbian novels by Anne Bannon (published in the 1960s by Volute Books, then reprinted in the 1980s by Naiad Press) exemplifies this pattern.

Chapter 11 | The Rest of the World in Love

1. Ethel Spector Person, *Dreams of Love and Fateful Encounters: The Power of Romantic Passion* (New York: W. W. Norton, 1988), 286.

2. John Money, *Love and Love Sickness: The Science of Sex, Gender Difference, and Pair Bonding* (Baltimore: Johns Hopkins University Press, 1980), 67.

3. Bernard Murstein, *Who Will Marry Whom? Theories and Research in Marital Choice* (New York: Springer, 1976), 25.

4. Christine Downing, *Myths and Mysteries of Same-Sex Love* (New York: Crossroad Publishing, 1989), xvii

5. Carla Golden, "Diversity and Variability in Women's Sexual Identities," and Rebecca Shuster, "Sexuality as a Continuum: The Bisexual Identity," in *Lesbian Psychologies: Explorations and Challenges*, ed. Boston Lesbian Psychologies Collective (Urbana: University of Illinois Press, 1987).

6. Golden, "Diversity and Variability," 31.

7. Susan Krieger, "Lesbian Identity and Community: Recent Social Science Literature," *Signs: Journal of Women in Culture and Society* 8 (1982): 91–108, and *The Mirror Dance: Identity in a Women's Community* (Philadelphia: Temple University Press, 1983).

8. Golden, "Diversity and Variability"; Sarah Pearlman, "The Saga of Continuing Clash in Lesbian Community, or Will an Army of Ex-Lovers Fail?," in *Lesbian Psychologies: Explorations and Challenges*, ed. Boston Lesbian Psychologies Collective (Urbana: University of Illinois Press, 1987).

9. Barbara Pense, *Identities in the Lesbian World: The Social Construction of Self* (Westport: Greenwood Press, 1978); Julia Penelope Stanley and Susan Wolfe, *The Coming Out Stories* (Watertown: Persephone Press, 1980); Golden, "Diversity and Variability."

10. Golden, "Diversity and Variability." Nancy Chodorow's *The Reproduction of Mothering: Psychoanalysis and the Sociology of Gender* (Berkeley: University of California Press, 1978) thesis supports this position.

11. Robert Knight, "Introjection, Projection, and Identification," *Psychoanalytic Quarterly* 9 (1940): 340.

12. Murstein, *Who Will Marry Whom?* 26.

13. Lillian Rubin, *Intimate Strangers* (New York: Harper & Row, 1983); Person, *Dreams of Love*.

14. Lorrie Moore, "Community Life," *The New Yorker*, Sept. 30, 1991, 33–34.

15. Downing, *Myths and Mysteries*, xxi, xxii

Chapter 12 | Clinical Meanings and Further Directions

1. Ethel Spector Person, *Dreams of Love and Fateful Encounters: The Power of Romantic Passion* (New York: W. W. Norton, 1988), 291, 307.

2. See Ronald Bayer, *Homosexuality and American Psychiatry: The Politics of Diagnosis* (New York: Basic Books, 1981).

3. Sophie Freud Lowenstein, "Understanding Lesbian Women," *Social Casework* 61 (1980): 37–38.

4. Stephen Morin, "Heterosexual Bias in Psychological Research on Lesbianism and Male Homosexuality," *American Psychologist* 32 (1977): 629–36.

5. Betty Berzon, *Permanent Partners* (New York: E. P. Dutton, 1988), 329.

6. See, for example, Philip Blumstein and Pepper Schwartz, *American Couples* (New York: William Morrow, 1983).

7. Abby Wolfson, "Toward the Further Understanding of Homosexual Women," *Journal of the American Psychoanalytic Association* 35 (1987): 165–73.

Index

BEVERLY BURCH received her doctorate from the California Institute for Clinical Social Work in Berkeley, where she is a clinical consulting faculty member. She also teaches at New College of California and is the author of a number of papers on both object relations theory and lesbian psychology. She maintains a private practice in Oakland.